To Brian,
Something to
think about!
Eric (signature)

THE
PROCRASTINATOR'S
GUIDE TO WILLS AND
ESTATE PLANNING

by Eric G. Matlin,
Attorney at Law

Ozanam Publishing

PAPER BACK

3nd Edition

ISBN # 978-0-9912462-6-7

Publisher's Note
This publication is designed to provide entertainment, along with accurate and authoritative information in regard to the subject matter covered. It is sold with the understanding that the publisher is not engaged in rendering legal, accounting, or other professional services. If you require legal advice or other expert assistance, seek the services of a competent professional.

A Note on Grammar
In this book, I followed the option of using plural pronouns *they*, *them* as singular nouns (*someone, anyone, a person, an individual, a client, a lawyer,* etc.), to keep them gender neutral.

I wrote the first edition of this book in 2004, published by New American Library division of Penguin Group, USA.

AUTHOR'S NOTE AND ACKNOWLEDGMENTS

This book is written for you, one of millions of Americans who *know* they need estate planning but who, using one excuse or another, never quite get around to starting or finishing it. Procrastination can—and *must*—be overcome.

My goal is to help you tackle the procrastination that's kept you—and continues to keep you—from completing one of the most critical responsibilities you have to your family, your friends, and your favorite causes and charities—as well as to yourself.

Some essential concepts of estate planning are relatively simple, and I've tried to be thorough and straightforward in those areas. Other complex concepts, which I don't regard as essential to the purposes of this book, are described in the leanest terms possible. Entire books can be, and in many cases have been, devoted to those subjects.

While I strive to learn from my mistakes in both my personal and my professional life, as a human being, I do make them. *Do not rely exclusively* on what you read in *The Procrastinator's Guide*. You will still have to consult an attorney, but reading these pages may help you go into the lawyer's meeting feeling more centered.

If you notice an ambiguity in these pages or a flat-out mistake, in either grammar or law, I will be grateful if you contact me via the Matlin Law Group website: www.MatlinLawGroup.com.

Dedicated to my loving wife, Glo.

I thank my law partners, my associate attorneys, my managers, and the rest of my staff at Matlin Law Group, P.C., whose dedication allows me the time luxury of writing a book or two (the other book being *Not Dead Yet, so plan your estate,* which uniquely includes a book-within-a-book graphic novel, enhancing the educational experience of those who learn better visually).

Thanks also to psychologist Thomas D. Yarnell, Ph.D., for his insights regarding procrastination, and to everyone else quoted in *The Procrastinator's Guide.*

Finally, I acknowledge all of the help, love, and accumulated knowledge from my family, friends, clients, colleagues, heroes, inspirations, and passing acquaintances of all races, faiths, and cultures, those still here and those of blessed memory. ●

CONTENTS

CHAPTER 1

The (Needlessly) High Cost of Procrastination

"Procrastination is the thief of time."
—Edward Young, *Night Thoughts*

If you're one of those people who just can't seem to get around to planning your estate, you're not alone. According to a Caring.com survey cited by AARP, approximately 60 percent of all American adults have no estate plan—no Will, no Trust, no powers of attorney, nothing at all. The remaining 40 percent? My experience during 25+ years of concentrating my law practice on estate planning tells me that most of them have estate plans that are so incomplete or out-of-date as to be little better than no plan at all.

Vast numbers of us delay everything from changing the oil in our cars to getting proper exercise. So why focus on estate planning in particular?

The answer is that *if you wait too long* to plan your estate or fail to update it periodically, your true intentions may be disregarded. You may *want* to cut taxes, you may *want* to avoid court costs and family aggravation, you may *want* to have a say in who will care for your child, and you may *want* to prevent your son from spending his inheritance buying rounds of drinks at his neighborhood tavern. But *if you wait too long*, that's too bad because you won't be able to do anything about these intentions.

It's time for you to take a deep breath and say to yourself, "I could die today." Putting off *thinking* about dying is not going to put off the actual event. In fact, you will probably never be as competent as you are right now. At the very least, you may never be *more* competent than you are now. If your attitude is "I'll be dead, so who cares?" this book is not for you. If you care about what happens to your money or your children or your partner when you die, keep reading.

If you wait too long, the estate you spent a lifetime building could be devastated by legal fees or taxes that might have been avoided. If you become incapacitated, your family may be required to make difficult decisions about your future without taking into account your preferences. Upon your death, your family can be dragged into a time-consuming court proceeding known as probate.

They'll be forced to accept the court's ruling, based on your state's intestacy law, about how your assets are to be divided, even if it means a relative you neither liked nor trusted gets a full share. Half siblings you don't even know are treated the same as full siblings, while step siblings you may have grown up with are completely ignored. Minor children could end up living with the last person you would have chosen as their guardian. If you are unmarried and have no blood relatives, the state might even get your estate, at the expense of friends or charities that could have benefited.

Search online "(state of your primary residence) intestacy" to see which relatives inherit your probate assets in the absence of a Will.

If you wait too long to plan your estate, you've fatally procrastinated, which is both risky and self-centered. If you tell yourself, "There's no rush, I'll take care of it soon," remember this: Estate planning is one task where the deadline often comes without warning—and there is no extension.

What's Your Excuse?

People procrastinate and delay estate planning for all sorts of reasons. Here are some of the most common excuses I've encountered, along with their rebuttals.

"I have so little money, it just isn't worthwhile for me."
It is true that protecting a large estate from taxes is one reason for estate planning, but it's certainly not the only reason or even the most important one. In a study reported by the Tax Policy Center of the Urban Institute and the Brookings Institution, it was projected that fewer than 1 of every 1,000 Americans dying in 2018 would have paid federal estate taxes.

More important than taxes for the vast majority of people, your estate plan will determine how your estate, regardless of its size, will be divided, and it will speak for you when you're unable to speak for yourself.

"I'm too young to worry about this."
No one likes to confront dying, so by failing to plan, you are able to avoid thinking about your death. Yet many people die before they reach "old" age. It's just another excuse to do nothing. Without an estate plan, your family's grief will be compounded by your failure to plan. If you have a family or other loved ones who depend on you, you have responsibilities, and you need to act with their welfare in mind. Grown-ups plan their estates.

One category of estate-planning procrastinators is the young family with young children, a big mortgage, and bigger term insurance policies. The beneficiary of the life insurance is the spouse. The contingent beneficiaries are the children, meaning that if both spouses die, leaving behind young children, they also leave a big mess—a guardianship estate, generating big legal fees with an end result that the children get the remaining money at age 18 with no strings attached—party time!

"I don't have a family, so estate planning is not an issue."

Estate planning isn't always about looking out for your family after you die—although that's usually an important part of it. Certain estate-planning tools can benefit you while you're still alive. For example, let's say you're in the hospital for an operation, and the doctor sees a potential complication that must be addressed—but you're under anesthetic. They need your permission to proceed, but you can't give it. What happens? Without a health-care power of attorney, you'll need a second operation. "Mr. Smith, the good news is that the six-hour operation was a success. The bad news is that as soon as you have recovered from the incision, we have to operate on you again."

With the right documents, a trusted agent acting under a power of attorney might be able to give consent for the second procedure. Chapter 5 examines this and other ways that an estate plan can help protect you during your lifetime.

Even if you don't have any dependents, you probably have some preference about who'll get your hard-earned assets when you die: a favorite cousin, a lifelong friend, a parent, a devoted employee, a charity. Without an estate plan, you've relinquished any voice in the matter. Make no mistake, if you don't do the planning, the court will do it for you. Lawyers are then involved to a greater extent than you would wish, and the court determines both how your property is controlled and who divides it.

"Thinking about it just makes me too anxious. I'd rather enjoy life."

While you might not enjoy the process, you may find that you get considerable satisfaction from the result. In fact, procrastinators looking for added motivation to get their estate planning done should consider this: You just might sleep better at night. Researchers have found that most procrastinators are not at all carefree about their inability to get things done. Unlike the fabled grasshopper that frittered away the summer without a care (only to find itself in dire straits come winter), procrastinators tend to suffer considerable anxiety about the crucial tasks they just can't seem to complete.

In fact, when people finish the estate-planning process, they are typically relieved. It doesn't matter whether it's a simple Will with powers of attorney or a complex set of documents designed to save an estate hundreds of thousands of dollars or even millions of dollars—you can feel good doing it!

To summarize: Everyone has to deal with estate matters at some point (whether it's you planning ahead of time or your heirs trying to do their best after your death), so why not do it now and not have to worry about it down the road? Once you finish, you can maximize its effectiveness by keeping it up-to-date, an easier process than starting it from scratch.

In most cases, it takes a little of your time and requires a legal expense—both modest costs for the peace of mind you'll gain. Taking care of this vitally important personal business before any emergency arises allows you to clear your mind so that you can turn your attention toward the more enjoyable facets of life . . . like cleaning the garage or having a root canal.

A Call to Action!

If this book gathers dust on your bookshelf (metaphysically, in the case of an e-book) without being acted on, then your good intentions in making this purchase will have failed. My goal is to help you do the appropriate amount of estate planning as your circumstances require. I have included thirteen "Action Plans" in this book, one for every chapter, which offer concrete instructions that will get you moving in the right direction, often within a defined time frame. I would suggest that as you sit down to read this, you bookmark certain passages or pages. Especially mark any action plans that require completion. If you intend to read this in one sitting, you are probably setting yourself up to fail. Take your time, but keep moving through the steps suggested.

A reasonable time horizon for finishing your estate plan starting from the time you begin this book is about one to three months (in other words, at least one action plan a week). The longer you go past that time frame, the less likely it is that you will ever finish. ●

Action Plan One: Let's Get Started!

This is an easy one and should be done immediately!

1. Grab a pen or a pencil and some notepaper or start taking notes on your computer or other electronic device. Use whatever works best for you. Think about some of the reasons that—even before reading this book—you already know you need an estate plan. Jot down some of your estate-planning hot buttons.

2. Pull out your calendar and mark a preliminary deadline for completing your estate plan. Over the next week, tell others about the deadline you have set for yourself in tackling your estate plan.

CHAPTER 2

Understanding Procrastination and Overcoming It

"To know what needs to be done, and then to do it, comprises the whole philosophy of practical life."—William Osler

Procrastination is the chronic postponement of necessary tasks—generally those considered difficult or unpleasant. We waste so much time trying to avoid these tasks that our failure in doing them is assured.

All of us put off an unpleasant task at some point in our lives. Occasional and short-term delays aren't necessarily disastrous. The real trouble comes when repeated procrastination begins to have a negative effect on your life.

According to numerous academic studies during the last 100 years, something like one-half of the population cause themselves some sort of loss through procrastination, and more than one-quarter experience chronic and debilitating procrastination.

Without being overly statistical, we are talking about tens of millions of people, illustrating why procrastination has been called the nation's single most common time-management problem. For those with a serious problem, procrastination causes considerable anxiety, leading to decreased personal productivity. The anxiety itself becomes the biggest roadblock to completing the task.

The Top Twelve

Below is my top-twelve list of the most common reasons that people delay estate planning. What is your reaction to each of these reasons? Do any sound familiar to you?

12. **Most people don't like to think about death or money.** Wills and Trusts force you to confront mortality and money, two issues that can be difficult to face. This is particularly true if you are healthy and don't feel you have much money.

11. **Estate planning is something most people are unfamiliar with or feel uncomfortable about.** Because you don't know much about estate-planning documents, you may experience anxiety or struggle with feelings of inadequacy when confronted with the subject. You know how to be a good plumber or schoolteacher or police officer or how to run a restaurant, but you don't know estate planning.

10. **There's no hard-and-fast deadline.** Many people can't accomplish anything until a deadline looms. But when it comes to Wills, Trusts, and powers of attorney, there is nothing on your calendar telling you when you will need it. The final deadline often comes without warning.

9. **It's not much fun.** True, but life isn't always fun, especially if you are an adult. If you need fun, plan a party to celebrate finishing your estate plan.

8. **People hate lawyers.** But not all lawyers deserve this animosity; you can find a good one you can relate to.

7. **People are afraid of massive amounts of paper.** If you understand the paperwork, it becomes less intimidating. Be prepared to ask questions about anything you don't understand.

6. **You won't live to see the largest benefits of your estate plan.** The main beneficiaries will be your heirs. It can be difficult to devote yourself to this task until you accept your family's priorities as your own.

5. **It might mean making decisions that could arouse negative feelings in loved ones.** Maybe you're concerned your family will be angry when they learn the details of your estate plan.

4. **The size of the job can be daunting.** Estate planning can be, but isn't necessarily, a big, time-consuming task. The perceived enormity of the task can prevent some people from even starting the job.

3. **Not doing your estate planning can be a form of passive-aggressive behavior.** If you're not happy with your future heirs, failing to complete necessary Wills or Trusts can be a subconscious way to punish them.

2. **Some people just like to live for the moment.** Some procrastinators simply can't—or won't—force themselves to pass up short-term pleasure and sit down to complete their estate planning, even if on some level they understand that doing so will provide them with far greater long-term satisfaction.

1. **Guilt feeds upon itself.** The real number-one excuse for not doing an estate plan, when you know you need one, is the wall built from guilt caused by putting off estate planning. This adds to any depression you might have about procrastinating in other areas of your life and leads, ironically, to further delay. If you can't move on from that state, a psychologist or a counselor who has experience working with procrastinators might help you.

All of these reasons to delay are perfectly understandable—but that doesn't make them any less dangerous or counterproductive. Fortunately, it is possible to use your natural fears to your benefit.

You know that doing nothing can make your worst fears come true. But whatever you fear about estate planning, the danger from your own inaction will always be greater. Just weigh the very real dangers of delay against the fear of thinking about money or mortality, and you might discover that doing your estate plan is easier not only in the long term, which is obvious, but also in the short term because the whole subject can then be put behind you.

Why We Procrastinate

We waste so much time trying to avoid difficult and unpleasant tasks that we set ourselves up for failure. Clinical psychologist Thomas D. Yarnell, Ph.D., has studied the subject of procrastination extensively. According to Dr. Yarnell, there are two major causes of procrastination:

- *Avoidance:* We procrastinate to avoid overwhelming, difficult, or unpleasant tasks and to avoid change.
- *Fear and anxiety:* We procrastinate because of our fear of failure, fear of success, fear of criticism, fear of making mistakes, and fear of rejection.

Let's cut to the chase. Here is a short list of techniques inspired by Dr. Yarnell that you can follow now to end procrastination and start this ball rolling. Since we are not all the same, Dr. Yarnell's advice is to keep the suggestions that work for you and forget the rest. The techniques will help you as you complete the action plans in this book, and when you have finished your estate plan, these tips will help you finish other tasks that have been delayed by procrastination.

1. Do the easiest part first so you can get started. Once you are moving, it's easier to continue.
2. Next, take the tasks you find most unpleasant or difficult and break them down into small steps to then be tackled one at a time.

3. Give yourself a deadline, and let others know it.
4. Get help. There is no rule that you must do everything yourself. For example, much of the information gathering needed in chapter 3 could be delegated to other people, such as your banker, broker, insurance agent, and so on. Make a very specific list of those you can call on.
5. Get organized so you can take advantage of momentum. There is nothing worse for a procrastinator than to get started, only to discover that you don't have everything you need to complete the task. You then have to stop, get the necessary materials or information, and start again. Get organized, get started, and keep going until you finish.
6. Use this book! I have broken up the task of estate planning into component pieces. If you take this book chapter by chapter, you'll find that no single task is overwhelming.

HOW TO DEFEAT PROCRASTINATION

Do unpleasant tasks first and get them over with.

Overcoming Estate-Planning Procrastination

While there are do-it-yourself Will and Trust form books, software packages, and online services, they can be confusing for the average person and a poor option for anyone who varies from what the author, the designer, the service, or the app believes to be a "normal" or "average" person. Moreover, it can be a waste of time or worse to attempt the admittedly complex task of estate planning without the assistance of an expert.

There might be little things an estate-planning lawyer will notice that are missing from a form document. For example, most estate-planning attorneys use an attestation clause (affidavit) at the end of a Will that allows the Will to be validated without the necessity of bringing the witnesses to testify that they saw you sign the document. Without such a clause, the witnesses may have to testify. Some form books, even some marketed to lawyers, leave out this simple affidavit or put it in a separate section, where it might be overlooked.

Estate planning can be a complicated process, but if the complexities of the process are holding up your estate plan, there is a simple, two-step solution to your problem:

First, use this book to help you sort through the issues of estate planning, get organized, and understand your options. If you walk into a meeting with an estate-planning attorney without having done any information gathering and background work on your own, your estate plan may not be as good as it could have been if you had initially invested the time to understand the concepts involved and to get organized.

Second, hire an estate-planning attorney. The right attorney can help you get motivated and move forward. Estate-planning attorneys have dealt with many or all of the issues that are likely to confront you. They not only understand the laws, but also know how to make the laws work best for you. They have dealt with different family situations and dynamics and have assisted their clients in overcoming procrastination.

REAL-LIFE STORIES

Sean and Arielle are in their forties and have children of ages 16, 14, and 8. Their form of estate-planning procrastination is common: While they had relatively little trouble determining who would handle their assets, they could not decide on a guardian for the kids. Their attorney was able to convince them that even an imperfect decision was better than no decision at all.

REAL-LIFE STORIES

How? By pointing out to them that if they failed to make a choice, not only would the decision be out of their hands, it would be totally out of their children's hands as well.

The two older children were old enough that the clients wanted them to have a say in the guardianship decision. At the time of the Will, however, there were too many unresolved factors for Sean and Arielle to impose a binding decision. Thus, the final document included language to the effect that any guardianship decision should be made in consultation with the children. They also discussed the fact that without proper planning, their children might not only be left without their parents, but also without their siblings. So the document noted that Sean and Arielle strongly desired that their children not be separated. The prospect of leaving their children without one another in homes they didn't like was enough to spur the couple to action.

If you're someone who avoids attorneys and attorneys' fees whenever possible, consider that hiring an estate-planning attorney isn't like hiring most other lawyers. Usually, an attorney is hired when it's necessary to go to court. Estate-planning attorneys are hired, at least in part, to keep your family out of court. And while any dealing with an attorney is likely to cost you money, the odds are good that an estate-planning attorney will, in the end, save you more in attorney costs than they charged as a fee—possibly much more.

Don't let a dislike of lawyers cause you to delay your estate planning. In the next chapter, we'll discuss the best way for a procrastinator to hire the right lawyer. ●

Action Plan Two: Ask Yourself
Some Tough Questions

1. Write down some of the reasons that you have procrastinated in doing your estate plan.
2. Envision the mess that could be created if you died today. If you are able to, write down a few of the worst scenarios that you can imagine if this were to happen.
3. Preliminarily, answer the question, "Is this something I can do on my own, or should I hire an attorney?" If you think you have already decided to do estate planning on your own, put another entry into your calendar for six weeks from now. If you have not made substantial progress by then, speak to a lawyer within two weeks after that. Put that deadline into your calendar as well.
4. List, in order of importance, all the things that matter most to you in the world. Most people with families put their spouse and children near the top of such a list. If that's true of your list, ask yourself: Do your actions square with your stated values? If your family means that much to you, shouldn't you ignore your own idiosyncrasies for a while and get your estate planning done?
5. If you can't resolve any difficult or sensitive family issues that seem to hinder your progress, put them aside for now. Look at it this way: No matter what decisions you eventually come to regarding your family, you're better off doing estate planning than not doing it. Yes, it can be difficult to decide whether or not to disinherit a child or precisely how to divvy up your estate, but dying without a Will only ensures

Action Plan Two: Ask Yourself
Some Tough Questions

that your voice will never be heard on the subject. Whatever your decision, it's always better that you decide something. If you change your mind later, you can change your documents.

CHAPTER 3

Getting Started

"The beginning is the most important part
of the work."
—Plato, *The Republic*

Getting started with the process of estate planning involves organizing your records and finding a way to complete the job. In this chapter, I'll help you get organized. In later chapters, I'll guide you along a path toward finishing the job.

I'll help you bring together all the information you're going to need to complete the plan—information about you, your family, and your finances.

I'll suggest a framework for getting the job done. For some, that might mean using a workbook, a computer program, or an online service designed for you to essentially do it yourself, but for most people it will mean selecting an attorney.

Nothing you'll need to do in this chapter requires any detailed knowledge of estate-planning tools or techniques, so there's no reason to put off these tasks. I'll break the process into small, manageable tasks and offer step-by-step guidance to prevent any confusion about how to proceed.

Precrastination?

A relatively new subject matter from a scholarly point of view, precrastination, was written about for the Association for Psychological Sciences based on experiments by a team led by David A. Rosenbaum, Ph.D., psychology professor at Pennsylvania State University. Precrastination describes how some people can waste energy on sub-goals that divert from the big picture of the job they are attempting to complete. No doubt, rushing through a job or focusing on the wrong items out of order can result in poor results, but if you follow the suggestions laid out in this book, your estate-planning efforts will suffer from neither procrastination nor precrastination.

Let's Get Organized

There are at least three good reasons to get all your personal and financial data together.

First, you can better determine what type of estate planning you need if you organize your personal finances.

Second, assuming you choose to hire an attorney to help you with your estate plan, the information you compile will make the task easier for both you and the lawyer. If you are prepared before walking in the door, you will get off to a better start—and possibly a lower attorney's bill as well.

Third, if something were to happen to you, this list could serve as a reference for your family in handling your affairs, even if it has no legal weight. One thing worse than leaving no estate plan is leaving no clue to the whereabouts of your assets. That's a nightmare.

HOW TO DEFEAT PROCRASTINATION

Get organized so you can take advantage of momentum. Nothing is worse for a procrastinator than to get started—at last—and discover you don't have everything you need to finish. You have to stop, find what you need, and then try to start again . . . days, weeks, or even years later. So get organized. Keep the momentum going until you finish.

The following questions should help you bring together most, if not all, information relevant to your estate plan. Some things you can answer without reference materials, but you'll need to do a little research to obtain all the information.

I've divided the work into four sections: personal data, financial data, fiduciary data, and other essential data. Do one section at a time.

Have everything you need for the project within arm's reach when you begin. This means fewer delays to search down missing pieces once you're under way, and it lowers the risk that you'll become distracted by other tasks while you're away from your desk.

For this part of the task, you may need a calculator. Also, grab your personal phone book, smartphone, or other access to your database so you have names, addresses, and telephone numbers of family and friends at your fingertips. Get any old Wills or Trusts and powers of attorney, if you have completed these types of documents in the past. And assemble account statements and other records relating to your possessions.

I encourage you to incorporate your answers into your favorite electronic device or print these pages and number your responses on paper or in a Word document. If a numbered item is irrelevant, just give it an "N/A."

Questionnaire Part One—Personal and Family Data

You'll need this important information about yourself:

Information Needed	Your Information
List your full name and any previous or other names you use; date of birth; mailing and email addresses; phone numbers, home, cell, and work.	
If you're married, list the same information for your spouse.	
If you or your spouse is not a U.S. citizen, what is your residency status? Generally, you will want to do your estate plan with an attorney licensed in the state of your principal residence.	
If applicable, list previous spouses' names, as well as when you were divorced or when the previous spouse died. If divorced and you or your current spouse have continuing obligations pursuant to a divorce agreement, make a copy of such agreement available for your lawyer meeting.	

Failure to consider divorce settlements when doing estate planning could result in your estate plan being contested or even invalidated. When meeting with a lawyer, be prepared to discuss with the lawyer some details of any of the breakups that were particularly adversarial

If you have children, provide information about each child, including full name, date of birth, current addresses (mailing and email), and phone numbers. For each child, note any special needs or diminished capacity, along with overall level of maturity as relating to money.	

This is a good time to start thinking about how you would like to treat your children in your Will/Trust. Will they all be treated the same? Does one have a special need that merits a different amount or different assets under different conditions?

Would you like to exclude any or all of your children from your estate? Be prepared to provide some details here. An estate-planning attorney can discuss specific options with you on this front, but it's best to have thought through your intentions in advance—disinheriting a child or another close family member shouldn't be a spur-of-the-moment decision.

Occasionally, parents who wish to disinherit a child will simply ignore the child in the plan. That's a mistake. Laws vary from state to state, but it's often necessary to explicitly state in your Wills or Trusts your intention not to include a child. You can leave a child nothing, but if you simply treat the child as if they don't exist, the child won't necessarily be cut out of your estate. They might be able to argue that you just forgot about them.

Do you or your spouse have children outside this marriage? If so, include all of the same information and analyses as above. Also, be prepared to discuss the relationship between your current spouse and previous children.	

To what degree would you like to include or exclude "other" children from your estate? Would you like them to be treated the same as your children from your current marriage? Differently? Even if these children have never been part of your life—or your current family doesn't even know about them—they should at least be mentioned somewhere, even if not in the main documents. Otherwise, your family could find out about them the hard way, when they challenge your Will after you're gone.

If you have any deceased children, make a note of it. It is particularly important to the estate-planning process if a deceased child had descendants.	

If you have grandchildren or great-grandchildren, you need pretty much all the same information that you listed for the children and, in addition, who is descended from whom. If you do have descendants beyond your children, do you want to make bequests to any of them independent of the bequests being made to your children?	

Are any grandchildren or great-grandchildren being treated differently from the others—or do you intend to cut any out of your estate? If so, provide the details.

Would you prefer to divide your assets among your children's families or so that every grandchild gets the same amount? For example, if you have two children, one with one child and one with four, is your estate still divided in two, with a 50 percent share going to each child together with their family?

If your estate is large enough that some of it will likely filter down to the next generation, this thought process can be important. Most people look to their children's generation, but some look further into the future in making this decision. Only you can decide what is most fair and will reflect your desires.

Do you have parents, siblings, stepchildren, nieces and nephews, other relatives, or close friends you wish to have included in your estate plan? If so, list the same information and analysis as above.	
If you wish anyone other than an intestate heir to inherit some portion of your estate, you must have an estate plan—if you die without an estate plan, these intended beneficiaries will often be cut out entirely, depending on which state you live in. Intestacy is purely by formula.	
Do you wish to include any charitable organizations as beneficiaries? If so, list names, addresses, and the EIN number, if you have it. Any special requests or limitations as to how the money is used?	

If you know what you want to leave to a charity and the specific purpose of the gift, indicate this also—your lawyer might suggest strategies for leaving assets in a way that optimizes the gift from everyone's perspective.

Are any of your beneficiaries in a position where you prefer they not take direct control of the assets you intend to leave them? In the case of minors, you will typically want to postpone control of their inheritance. It is up to you to decide at what ages your beneficiaries should control their shares of your estate. You also can restrict control of assets for adults.	

If you would like to explore this possibility, explain briefly why you think it might be a good idea to restrict control of assets left to these people—for example, have they always been irresponsible with money? Do they have a history of substance abuse? Are they in a profession with a high risk of being sued?

Also, give some idea how much control you wish the inheritors to have—should they have free access over some portion of the assets but not all? Should they have no access, except for certain purposes? Do they need someone watching over every withdrawal?

There's no need to be precise here; just jot down some ideas. Failure to plan ahead in this area means that every adult inheriting from you will receive their share without limitations soon after your death.

Is there any person you wish to exclude from your estate plan who otherwise might expect to be included? Is there any person whom you fear may try to thwart your wishes? Is there anyone you feel may try to influence your personal finances a little more than you would prefer? Jot down brief details, but be prepared to talk about the situation more extensively with your attorney.	

It is a good idea to explain to your lawyer why you're choosing to completely exclude an individual, but be dispassionate in your Will or Trust and don't put language in there that may be libelous, such as "John is a thief, and that is why I am disinheriting him," unless you can point to a theft conviction. Even then, I would advise leaving such language out. Even in my rookie lawyer days, I knew enough to steer around such dangerous language, but I might have added something like "For reasons best known to John, he is receiving no part of this estate." Because of my acquired wisdom, I now prefer simply to say, "For all purposes of this Will (or Trust), John shall be deemed to have predeceased me leaving no descendants." You don't need a reason to leave your assets where you wish, but it helps if your lawyer knows at least part of the backstory.

If strife can be expected, there are steps that can be taken to reduce any troublemakers' chances of success. This can be a difficult topic to consider because no one likes to think about the relatives we don't get along with or those who simply can't be trusted. But it's far better to confront such matters now than it is to leave your heirs in a battle royale after you're gone.

Warning: Dying without proper estate-planning documents in place likely means that each of your children will receive the same amount from your estate, even if one of them has spent his life in faithful service to the family business, and another hasn't called you for the last twenty years.

The law does not attempt to determine what each child deserves. If you haven't bothered to provide guidance through an estate plan, your spouse and children will inherit according to the preset formula under your state law.

Also note that if you have a spouse or children, no one else is likely to get a thing unless you spell it out.

Congratulations! You've finished this section. Take a break, and give yourself a reward. Feel better knowing you are one step closer to completing your estate plan.

Questionnaire Part Two—Assets, Liabilities, and Other Financial Data

You probably know the approximate value of your estate. But with estate planning, details are essential. Of particular interest: If you're married, you'll have to specify the ownership details of each asset mentioned on the list. That means spelling out whether an item is owned by you, either individually or through a Trust; owned by your spouse—again, individually or through a Trust; or owned jointly by the two of you together.

An asset's value is not what you paid for it, but what it is worth *today* on the open market, "fair market value." For most items of tangible personal property, including automobiles, fair market value is likely to be less than the amount you paid, but antiques, collectibles, artwork, and real estate may have increased in value, sometimes dramatically. In some instances, you might need to obtain a professional appraisal to establish fair market value.

Do you own real estate? Provide the following information for each property that you own or any property in which you hold a partial interest. All real estate, starting with the primary residence, needs the following information:

Primary residence	
Address	
Approximate value	
If there is an outstanding mortgage or another lien, how much?	
How is the title held?	

List the same information for other real estate holdings.

Other real estate holdings	
Address	

Approximate value	
If there is an outstanding mortgage, how much?	
How is the title to this property held?	

If you have a copy of the deed or other conveying instrument, that is an item to bring to an attorney meeting, but don't knock yourself out looking for it because all deeds must be recorded anyway to be legal, making them part of the public record and accessible for a small fee from a county clerk or a recorder of deeds.

Your property-tax assessment might be a useful guide to the value of a piece of property. Or just ask a real estate agent, who will usually be more than willing to give you an unofficial appraisal, either because they are nice or because they hope to get your listing someday.

If you fail to do the proper planning, particularly if you own any out-of-state property, your heirs will be required to go through additional legal hassles.

Do you have life insurance? List the following information for each policy.

What type of insurance is it? Whole life, universal, variable, or term?	
If term, how many years of level premiums remain?	
Who are the owner and the beneficiary (including all contingent beneficiaries) of each policy? If a Trust, the lawyer will need a copy of that Trust agreement.	
What is the cash value of each policy?	
What is the death benefit of each policy?	
If you're a veteran, do you have GI life insurance? Please list the policy number, the death benefit, and the beneficiaries.	

Make a list of any accidental death benefits arising from such sources as motor clubs, group health insurance policies, and credit card companies. These should not be included in the accounting of your net worth, but it may be worthwhile to list them here because they might be payable to a beneficiary, and you don't want them to fall through the cracks and be overlooked by your family.

What is the source of the accidental death benefit?	
What are the appropriate membership, policy, or credit card numbers?	

What other financial assets do you own, and what are their current values?

Asset	Financial institution, account numbers, interest rates, maturities, approximate value
Money market accounts Savings and checking accounts Certificates of deposit Credit union accounts U.S. savings bonds Treasury bonds, notes and bills Municipal and corporate bonds GNMAs and other U.S. agency–issued notes receivable Mortgages owned (this doesn't mean mortgages you owe, but those owed to you) Mutual funds Stocks, as well as any other brokerage accounts not included elsewhere on the list Annuities. Assemble the most recent statements.	
Retirement plan assets—IRAs (regular, rollovers, and Roths), 401(k)s, 403(B)s, 457 Plans, SEPs, and other "qualified" retirement plans. List the beneficiary and the contingent beneficiary of each plan, if any. List beneficiaries, primary and contingent. Also, Health Savings Accounts (HSAs). Private business entities, such as sole proprietorships, limited partnerships, family corporations (C and S), and limited liability companies.	

It's a good idea to keep track of your cost basis, which is the amount you originally paid for the asset. When you sell the asset, the cost basis may be necessary to determine your gain or loss on the sale of the asset, which is reported on your annual income-tax return.

These details won't necessarily have much effect on your typical estate plan, but it's good to have the information handy for your family in case someday they need to take over your affairs. An up-to-the-minute valuation of each account isn't required. Just get the ballpark figure from a recent account statement for each, and be sure you haven't omitted any accounts. This information may also be important if you make a gift of any of these assets during your lifetime.

Tangible Personal Property

Make particular note of special items, such as valuable collections, antiques, art, or jewelry.

Description	Value/Comments	Location	Beneficiary

Figuring out the fair market value of your possessions doesn't need to be a complicated process; you are trying to determine a ballpark estimate. In most cases, there is no need to have your assets professionally appraised at this point, and you don't need to be concerned with relatively minor personal possessions. Start with those items you know or believe to have a fair market value of $1,000 or more.

With respect to other personal possessions, such as consumer electronics, appliances, furniture, and clothing, there's no need for a complete listing. For purposes of estate planning, the values assigned to such items are roughly akin to what you might pay for them at a garage sale, so don't let yourself get bogged down trying to decide a fair market value for an eight-year-old toaster oven. Assign the personal property a nominal value as a group, which for most people is usually not more than a few thousand dollars.

If you have a particular beneficiary in mind for any special item of personal property, indicate that, too. For example, perhaps there's a musically gifted grandchild who would appreciate your piano or items with special sentimental value if you know whom you want to have them.

Do you own titled personal property, such as cars, boats, and airplanes?

Description	Value/Comments	Location	Beneficiary

Do you own prepaid cemetery plots or funeral expenses, season tickets to sporting events that may be valuable. Copyrights, patents and other potential sources of future royalties or other earnings?

In general, don't forget to include any item of value, tangible or intangible, located where your heirs might not think to look because it is either hidden for safety or not kept in your house. If you have a bank safe-deposit box, provide the details, and make sure one of your heirs will have access to it upon your death or disability (see chapter 7).

Now total the value of your assets from this first part of Questionnaire Two, including the cash value of your life insurance, but not including the life insurance death benefit, and enter the number here: $_____. Add the amount of the life insurance death benefit here: $_____.

Are you the plaintiff or the defendant in any ongoing lawsuits? If there is a good chance that these could result in additional assets being added to your estate or a judgment against you reducing your estate, your estate plan should take this into consideration. Describe the cause of action, and list the lawyer's contact information.

Description	Comments	Attorney or Legal Firm

Do you anticipate inheriting money or other assets? Obviously, if you have not yet received an expected inheritance, the projected receipt of the inheritance should be noted but not figured into your assets or net worth

Description	Amount	Source

Of course, you may not know all of the details in advance, but provide as accurate an estimate as possible. Do you know how the inheritance will be transferred to you? Is there a Trust, or will the property pass directly via a joint tenancy or beneficiary designation? It can be difficult to discuss details of inheritances with your parents or with anyone who might have you in their Will, but there can be sizable benefits to doing so. For example, if you have a high net worth, you may want to coordinate your estate plan with that of your parents and even with those of your children, if they have a high net worth, to limit estate taxes and for other reasons.

Whenever there is a major change in your financial situation, marital status, state of residence, or intended beneficiaries, your estate plan must be reexamined.

What are your liabilities? List the following information.

Description of Liability	Dollar Amount
Amount of mortgages and other liens and the properties they relate to	
The balance on student loans	
The balance on automobile loans	
The balance on credit card balances, other notes payable	
The margin balance in brokerage accounts	
Any outstanding judgments against you	
Other liabilities, in excess of $1,000.	

Total Liabilities: $_____.

What is your estimated net worth (assets, including cash value of life insurance) minus liabilities)?

$_____ Here, add the life insurance death benefit: $_____.

Don't worry about counting every last dollar because your net worth is going to change between now and the time you die. Calculate your estimated net worth, and don't leave out any major financial assets or liabilities.

Do not include in your net worth any accounts for which you are a custodian for a minor, such as Uniform Gifts to Minors Act (UGMA) or Uniform Transfer to Minors Act (UTMA) accounts, unless you have named yourself as custodian (which, as discussed in chapter 11, may not be a good idea, as it may subject the account to probate upon your death). Also, do not include any account for which you act as trustee if you were not the grantor and you do not have a general power of appointment over the account (see the glossary for an explanation of these terms, or ask your attorney for details).

Have you filed any gift-tax returns during your lifetime? Has your spouse? Generally, you should have filed a gift-tax return if you ever made a gift of more than the annual exclusion amount, which is (in 2021) $15,000, to any person other than your spouse in any single year. A copy of any gift-tax returns filed may be useful information to the attorney when you meet her.

Congratulations! You've finished another section (well, a subsection, at least, but a big one!). Take a break. Reward yourself, as you promised you would do. And feel better knowing you are another step closer to completing your estate plan.

Questionnaire Part Three— Fiduciary Data

Fiduciaries are those persons or companies that will act on your behalf when you are unable to do so.

List a primary fiduciary and as many contingent (secondary and so on) fiduciaries as you need to feel comfortable with the roles these people will play on your behalf, along with contact information.

Role	"Name, address, and telephone number
Guardian of your minor children.	

It's important to discuss this role with anyone you select. If, in fact, they do not want your darlings, you need to know that up front and make a different selection. Otherwise, it can lead to guilt for the guardian turning your children away or a Cinderella, wicked step-parent scenario.

Agent for health care to make medical and other personal decisions for you if you are incapacitated.	
Agent for property (finances), who can pay your bills and has contractual authority on your behalf upon your incapacity.	
Executor for your Will. To the extent you avoid probate, discussed in chapter 7, this can be a relatively minor job.	
Trustee for your Trusts. If you have a Trust, this is the most important financial role in most instances, although the executor, the agent under the power of attorney, and the trustee may be the same person wearing different hats.	

If you haven't selected these people, jot down the names of those who seem like they might be appropriate. We'll talk about how to select fiduciaries in chapters 5, 7, and 8.

Questionnaire Part Four— Other Essential Data

Do you have a CPA or a financial adviser? Supply contact information for all such persons and their company affiliations.

Adviser	Company name, address, and telephone number	Function

If you hire an attorney to draft your estate plans, they may need to work together with your other financial professionals.

Where do you keep your important documents, such as insurance policies or previous estate plans? Who has access to your documents and essential passwords?

Document	Location	Name, address, and telephone number of person with access

We'll discuss the proper place to store such documents in chapter 13. For now, it's important that someone else knows where the documents are stored and has access to them in an emergency.

What are your wishes for burial, cremation, funeral, or memorial plans?

Is there anything else you consider important to your estate-planning needs? Do you have any other concerns that should be addressed? ●

DID YOU HAVE TROUBLE GETTING THROUGH THIS LIST?

In a perfect world, every client would walk into a lawyer's office with all the necessary information ready to go. But if gathering this information is causing you to procrastinate

DID YOU HAVE TROUBLE GETTING
THROUGH THIS LIST?

about your estate plan, there are only two or three things that are essential to have with you when you finally show up:

1. If you are old school, your address book, so you can provide names and addresses of beneficiaries who will receive your assets and of fiduciaries who will act on your behalf if you die or become incapacitated. If you are more modern, just bring your smartphone or tablet with all the contact information for these people.

2. A rough idea of your financial situation, including an estimate (say, within a few hundred thousand dollars) of the value of your estate, the size of your IRA or other retirement plan assets, and the death benefits of any life-insurance policies you own.

3. If you can easily obtain them, any prior and perhaps now out-of-date Wills or other estate-plan documents. If you have a previous Trust or have access to one you are the beneficiary of, that will be fairly essential for any meaningful get-acquainted meeting with an attorney.

Action Plan Three: Congratulations,
You're Making Real Progress!

You deserve a treat!

If you have done (or delegated, with a calendar notation to follow up with the person you assigned the job to) most of the work in this chapter, you should feel good about your progress.

Reward yourself! Take a hot bath; pour yourself something delicious; pick up the novel that you put aside to read this book; get out in the sun and smell the flowers; plant yourself a garden if you have no flowers; veg out in front of the television; take a nap—whatever works for you!

CHAPTER 4

Getting Help . . . or Doing It Yourself?

"A man who dies without a Will has lawyers for his heirs." —Anonymous

Now that you've completed your lists, you have a decision to make: Do you get professional help by hiring an attorney—or buy a book or computer software to help you draft the documents yourself? You can also obtain legal services online.

No law says you must use an attorney to create an estate plan. Doing it yourself is cheaper, but beware: You might just get the value of what you paid. Although many of the resources to do it yourself are detailed, your unique situation may be different from the models presented. And who will answer your questions? Who will catch your mistakes? A single oversight or error could cost you or your heirs more—much more—than a lawyer would have charged for a proper estate plan.

A COMPROMISE

If you want to save some money but still assure yourself of a quality estate plan, here's a compromise option:

A COMPROMISE

Do your own estate plan, then pay an estate-planning attorney on an hourly basis to review the work.

Some people, generally those willing to invest considerable time in understanding some of the intricacies of estate planning, manage to do a decent job with a do-it-yourself kit. For them, a lawyer might need a few hours to review their homemade plan and possibly recommend minor changes. Of course, it can take much longer if the do-it-yourself plan was not properly prepared.

The do-it-yourself approach is often a poor idea for procrastinators. Before you ante up for the book or the software, ask yourself whether you're really likely to use the program once you have it. Have you purchased similar do-it-yourself kits in the past? Did you use them? Do-it-yourself income tax–reporting programs, similar in some ways to estate-planning kits, come with federally imposed deadlines that can motivate the procrastinator. Estate planning has few deadlines that arrive without irreparable repercussions.

Procrastinators may get stuck at this critical point because they have little, no, or only negative experiences with lawyers and know even less about where and how to find an estate-planning lawyer.

HOW TO DEFEAT PROCRASTINATION: DON'T GET STUCK!

Keep moving ahead by finishing this chapter before you do anything else. Break unpleasant or difficult tasks into small steps, and tackle them one at a time.

There's nothing wrong with a little caution: Selecting the right lawyer is a crucial part of this process, and because you'll be sharing some very personal details with the lawyer, you'll certainly want to find someone you can relate to and trust.

Don't let caution turn into stagnancy. Follow the strategies outlined in this section, and you should be able to find a lawyer suited to you and to the estate-planning task you've started.

Burger's Blunder

Just how tricky is estate planning for a layman or even a lawyer who does not concentrate his law practice in that area? U.S. Supreme Court Chief Justice Warren Burger, a prominent jurist but not an estate-planning professional, made a number of crucial errors when he wrote his own Will prior to his death in 1995. Justice Burger's Will:

- Failed to grant the executors powers to act independently of the court's supervision, so his heirs were forced to have the probate court approve every step of his estate's liquidation and distribution;
- Failed to waive bond or surety, which added insurance costs;
- Was not "self-proving"—that is, it didn't include a notarized affidavit by the witnesses that they signed in each other's presence—an oversight that most likely led to added court appearances and lawyers' fees and can also lead to the necessity of tracking down the witnesses to sign new affidavits or appear in court;
- Failed to take advantage of various techniques for reducing estate taxes; and
- Left his entire estate open to public scrutiny, like you and me. Anyone was able to contact the Arlington County, Virginia, probate court to obtain Justice Burger's complete probate file, including an inventory of his assets. Most families would prefer to keep these types of matters private.

LAST WILL AND TESTAMENT
OF
WARREN E. BURGER

I hereby make and declare the following to be my last will and testament.

1. My exeuctors will first pay all claims against my estate;

2. The remainder of my estate will be distributed as follows: one-third to my daughter, Margaret Elizabeth Burger Rose and two-thirds to my son, Wade A. Burger;

3. I designate and appoint as executors of this will, Wade A. Burger and J. Michael Luttig.

IN WITNESS WHEREOF, I have hereunto set my hand to this my Last Will and Testament this ___9th___ day of June, 1994.

Warren E Burger
_____
WARREN E. BURGER

We hereby certify that in our presence on the date written above WARREN E. BURGER signed the foregoing instrument and declared it to be his Last Will and Testament and that at this request in his presence and in the presence of each other we have signed our names below as witnesses.

[signature] residing at 120 'F' St, NW
Washington, DC

Alice M. Khu residing at 3041. Meeting. St
~~FARFAX VA~~ Falls Church, VA

SWORN TO AND SUBSCRIBED BEFORE ME THIS 9th
DAY OF ___June___ 19 94 *Constance Y. Ferguson*
NOTARY PUBLIC

CONSTANCE Y. FERGUSON
Notary Public, District of Columbia
My Commission Expires January 31, 1999

Probate caused a drain of at least $250,000 to $300,000 (in 1995 dollars) on Justice Burger's estate. When all the taxes and the legal costs were added up, they accounted for nearly half of his roughly $2 million estate—and the probate took more than three years. If Justice Burger had made the right moves, he could have saved hundreds of thousands of dollars and protected his privacy.

Get an Estate-Planning Lawyer

Justice Burger's story makes an obvious point: not every lawyer handles estate planning. Some states certify a legal specialty in estate planning. Certification ensures that the lawyer is taking regular classes on the subject. Because the laws governing estates change and evolve, taking classes can keep a lawyer fresh and up-to-date. However, many states do not certify an estate-planning specialty. As an Illinois lawyer, I can only say that I "concentrate my law practice on estate planning." If I were to say I'm an "expert" or an estate-planning "specialist," I would be reprimanded.

Even among lawyers who are submerged in estate planning, there are elite lawyers who concentrate not only on estate planning, but on the very latest cutting-edge tax techniques, and charge accordingly. In general, they're most appropriate for those with estates worth well into the tens of millions of dollars. If you are in that situation, such attorneys will probably be worth every penny you spend on their services. If that's your situation, insist that your lawyer call in the big guns, if needed—at least, as cocounsel.

What Will My Lawyer Do?

Estate-planning lawyers are not reinventing the wheel with completely new documents for every client. Estate-planning forms and reference materials for lawyers to use are often written by the Trust divisions of large, well-known banks or a particular state's continuing legal education forum. The firm I am associated with utilizes forms supplied by the Illinois Institute of Continuing Legal Education (IICLE), which are widely used in my geographic area.

An excellent estate-planning lawyer must do more than just fill in the blanks on the forms. To give good service, your lawyer must:

- Comprehend what each provision means and what its effects will be for you;
- Keep track of major developments in estate planning;
- Make modifications to the basic forms based on recurring situations;
- Understand your family dynamics, finances, and goals to the extent necessary to draft competent legal documents tailored to your needs; and
- Explain the documents to your satisfaction.

Finding the Lawyer Who Is Right for You

Here are five steps to take. It's possible you won't need all of them. Finding the right lawyer is as important as getting all of your family and financial information together, which you've already done. The information is ready to be put to work once you have a lawyer who is right for you.

1. Set a deadline for finding a lawyer. The process might take you a day or two, but it could take longer, so the best idea might be to set a target date as your deadline for having met with the attorneys to whom you were referred. Set a second deadline for making your decision. Once that's done, make an appointment, and remember to write it in your calendar.

2. Restrict yourself to lawyers who concentrate their practice on estate planning. It will dramatically reduce the number of lawyers whom you may choose among. You can go outside your immediate area to find a lawyer if you're willing to make the trip, but if you live near a state border, don't cross it. A lawyer practicing in one state might not be up on all the rules in another.

3. Network:
   - Ask your friends who they used to do their estate planning and whether they were pleased with the results. Stick to friends in roughly the same economic situation as yourself, and, of course, ask only those whose judgment you trust.
   - If your friends can't provide any recommendations, or if you've just moved and don't yet have any close friends in the region, ask your financial professionals. If you have an accountant, a financial planner, or a general-practice attorney, ask any or all of them whether they can provide leads.
   - Another promising resource is your bank. Ask to speak to a Trust officer or the bank manager.
     - If you still can't get a referral, call your state's bar association and ask for names. A list of state bar association phone numbers is available at the American Bar Association's website www.abanet.org/legalservices/public.html. Bar associations provide referrals as a free service.
     - Three more suggestions: Check guidebooks to attorneys such as the *Martindale-Hubble Law Directory* (www.martindale.com), available in the reference section of many public libraries; check out websites for "estate planning attorneys" in your geographical area; and finally, if you can find a telephone book, check the yellow pages.
4. Investigate costs and fee structures.

Once you've found an attorney who concentrates in estate planning, the next question you might ask may be: "How much is this going to cost me?"

That's a fair question. If the price is too high, it's best to find out as soon as possible and look for someone else. But most people have no clear idea how much the lawyer's services should cost them. Everyone's situation is different, and prices differ from region to region, so an appropriate fee can vary tremendously.

To give you a feel for what to expect, however, an average person in need of a plain-vanilla estate plan, including the standard documents, should expect to pay anywhere from $1,000 to $5,000. However, estates requiring complex estate-planning tools might reasonably cost $5,000 to $15,000 and much (much!) more. Such plans can save these estates millions of dollars in taxes.

Don't assume you'll receive inadequate service from a lower-cost attorney. Many competent attorneys concentrating their practice on estate planning have modest offices and low overhead. Many of these lawyers will do a great job for you at a reasonable price, particularly if there's nothing very unusual about your situation. Besides, not everyone is comfortable in fancy or pretentious law firm suites.

Many estate-planning lawyers offer a free consultation for prospective clients. Others may charge for the initial consultation but waive that fee once hired. Before your get-acquainted interview or initial consultation, confirm what the first meeting will cost.

Before agreeing to anything, you should ask the attorney for an estimated cost for the whole job. Otherwise, everyone's time might be wasted, and misunderstandings could result. Beyond the lawyer's hourly rate, you have a right to know up front how much your whole estate plan will cost, even if it is just an estimated range. Let the lawyer take a look at the information you've brought with you concerning your assets and your personal and family situation. That should help them estimate what your plan will require.

The cost of your estate plan may vary according to the amount of time the lawyer will spend on it. Many lawyers will charge a flat fee for drafting the documents and for advising you generally as to how your various assets should be structured, if restructuring is needed to avoid probate or reduce future estate taxes.

If you want the attorney involved in all aspects of that restructuring, such as filling out change-of-ownership or change-of-beneficiary forms, this will naturally add to the time and increase the cost of the estate plan.

Some lawyers charge a flat fee for estate planning, and you might get a fairly precise quote, but make sure that everything you will need for a complete plan is included in this fee. Some attorneys offer a flat fee for services that include only the barest bones, with many other components being added to the bill. After reading this book, you should have a good idea what components your plan will require. After being quoted a fee, don't be afraid to try to negotiate for a lower price, especially if you expect that your plan will be relatively simple and without any twists.

5. Size up the lawyer. The initial consultation offers you an opportunity to assess the attorney's personality, competence, and communication skills. Don't underestimate the importance of personality. Find someone with whom you can work efficiently, someone with whom you're comfortable discussing very intimate details of your family and finances. If you don't feel you click with a particular attorney, trust your instincts and keep searching.

Here are some other questions to ask yourself after your first meeting:

Question:	Yes	No	Your comments
Did they return your telephone calls or email communications promptly to your satisfaction?			
Did they listen to what you had to say and communicate their own thoughts in a manner that you were able to understand?			
Did they make you wait beyond the scheduled appointment time?			

How long have they been estate-planning attorneys?			
Can they provide references — either clients or financial-service professionals?			

Also consider calling your state bar to ask if any complaints have been filed against this attorney or whether they have ever been disciplined by the bar.

Some estate-planning attorneys belong to national marketing networks, which usually provide their own form documents to the attorney. Some of these networks are better than others. If you retain an attorney who is part of a national network, keep an eye out for two factors:

- First, since the network is likely to be national in scope, make certain the documents are not overly voluminous, in an attempt to comply with the laws of all states. You can ask to take a look at a sample set of documents to see how much extraneous material (items not applicable to the state in which you live) is included.

- Second, make sure you are dealing directly with the attorney who is writing the documents. Many financial planners take an interest in a client's complete financial picture and are involved in estate-planning aspects in a very positive way. But some financial planners position themselves as go-betweens, so that you may not even meet with a lawyer. What that does is add another layer of fees. Fee splitting between estate-planning lawyers and financial planners is prohibited in most states, but it is still happens. I'm talking about those free dinners offered by financial-service professionals partnered with an attorney, offering to teach you how to "Avoid Probate!"

Once you've made a decision, here's what to expect: Typically, in a relatively simple situation, an estate-planning attorney might meet with you once or twice before signing documents, in addition to your initial consultation. Expect each meeting to last between one and three hours or more, depending on the complexity of the plan, your personal concerns, and the attorney's level of detail in explanation. Ask all your questions. There is no such thing as a stupid question! A lawyer cannot competently draft estate-planning documents without a "meeting of the minds" between lawyer and client.

At a first meeting, you'll likely discuss your estate and intentions; at the second, you may review a draft of the estate plan and sign it; or you might have a third meeting to sign the documents. Of course, if you have a very complex plan, more communications will be needed.

As a reminder, here are the goals for your estate plan:
- To hold and ultimately dispose of your assets and provide for anybody dependent on you;
- To transfer your assets, upon your death, to the persons or the charities you've selected, under the conditions you've chosen, while minimizing costs such as probate and estate taxes; and
- To clearly state who will act on your behalf to carry out your wishes in the event of death and/or incapacity.

A complete estate plan for many people consists of these documents:
1. Revocable living Trust;
2. Will (a "pour-over Will" if used in conjunction with a revocable living Trust);
3. Power of attorney for property (finances);
4. Health-care directives (power of attorney for health care, perhaps a living Will, and sometimes a stand-alone HIPAA authorization);

5. Other documents—such as real estate deeds—that implement the plan.

Your estate-plan documents might be augmented by charitable or insurance Trusts, gifting programs, or other advanced techniques. We'll take a look at some of the key weapons in the estate-planning arsenal later on.

Once you begin the process, your lawyer should continue to provide you with the attention that you received initially. Do they still return your telephone calls and other communications promptly? The number-one reason people become dissatisfied with their lawyers and other service professionals is their failure to communicate in a reasonably prompt manner.

Some lawyers, being human, also procrastinate. If you feel your lawyer is not working diligently toward finishing your estate plan after beginning the process, communicate this to them, and, if necessary, begin the process again with a new lawyer.

Estate planning is often more art than an exact science because personalities and family dynamics are so important to estate planning. Five different lawyers may have five different approaches to the same situation, all of which may be valid. Even the same lawyer's work will evolve, so that the documents a lawyer might have prepared five or ten years ago are different in various ways than those drafted now. This does not make the old documents bad, but laws obviously change, and in many cases a lawyer may learn a few things on the practice road that will "tweak" documents for the better. ●

Action Plan Four: Let's Keep the Ball Rolling!

A five-step strategy for selecting your lawyer:

1. Today, call trusted friends and ask whether they can recommend an estate-planning lawyer.

2. If your friends can't help, by the end of the week find a lawyer through a referral from another professional, such as your CPA, banker, or insurance broker; or use a referral service, such as the state or local bar association. Check out lawyers online.

3. Call the lawyer(s) next Monday, and do a very brief preliminary interview. Do they concentrate their practice on estate planning? Do they offer a free or, at least, a reasonably priced initial consultation? Is their cost structure in line with what you feel is reasonable, given the complexity of your needs? Can they schedule a consultation at a time that fits your schedule?

4. Book an appointment and write it in your calendar. Make arrangements for child care (or bring your children, if it's okay with both you and the lawyer) or get some time off work if necessary.

5. Between now and then, complete this book so you're as prepared as possible.

CHAPTER 5

Looking Out for Yourself (Avoiding an Adult Guardianship)

"Even if you're on the right track, you'll get
run over if you just sit there."
—Will Rogers

Many people start the estate-planning process with their families in mind, thinking that all they need is a "simple" Will so that their assets will be divided properly after their death.

But most people don't realize just how much an estate plan can do for them while they're still alive—if they would just stop procrastinating and get the plan done.

Generally speaking, a well-crafted estate plan can benefit you during your lifetime in two ways: It can speak for you on matters of health care and finance when you are incapacitated and therefore unable to speak for yourself. It can also protect your assets against lawsuits and other threats.

If you've been procrastinating about estate planning because you feel so young and vital, look at it in a different light: it's a way to be prepared for the unexpected. A properly constructed estate plan can make a big difference if you:

- Have a serious accident or another misfortune that leaves you unable to look after your own assets,
- Need to have a medical decision made during an operation while you're under anesthesia,
- Develop a medical condition that leaves you unable to convey your wishes about your place of residence or medical care, or
- Suffer a sudden hopeless medical condition, are unable to communicate, and would like your opinion heard about the efforts made to keep you alive.

Let's examine those events and see what a well-crafted estate plan can do for you now.

Guardianship of the Person

If you become incapacitated, you are unable to speak for yourself, and you don't have the proper documents in place, there's a strong chance your medical care will be handled differently than you would want. Other people will be making life-and-death decisions for you, without the benefit of your input.

In this case, your family may be forced to go into court and initiate a "living probate" commonly known as a guardianship or a conservatorship (as opposed to a "death probate").

The court will appoint a guardian of the *person* with respect to your health-care matters (and a guardian for the *estate* to handle your financial affairs, which we'll cover a little later). In a guardianship of the person proceeding, the court appoints a guardian to make health-care and lifestyle decisions for you if you can no longer effectively communicate. For example, the court typically grants its appointed guardian authority to select a place of residence for you, which may mean a nursing home.

If you have an estate plan, you select your guardian, instead of the court. You also provide guidelines and instructions for your agent, reflecting your wishes.

Another problem with probate is the cost in time and money. When a person without a power of attorney for health care is kept alive in a hospital by life-sustaining machines, the family's decision to curtail such care might not be accepted until the family works its way through the time-consuming, potentially costly, and public probate court system to name a guardian. While some circumstances may allow for a quick guardianship resolution, others may drag on for years, especially if family members cannot agree on a course of action. Meanwhile, depending on your health insurance, hospital bills might be piling up alongside the legal bills.

Health-Care Directives

Estate-planning tools, known as "health-care directives" or "advance directives," ensure that even if you are unable to communicate, your philosophies regarding life-and-death decisions will be implemented. The most widely recognized health-care directives are:

• Powers of attorney (POA) for health care, which state your wishes and appoint someone to make choices regarding your treatment.

• Living Will, which simply states your philosophy regarding life-sustaining treatment within the context of a terminal illness.

The POA for health care and a living Will are based on the idea that adults have the absolute right to make their own medical-care decisions. This includes the decision to have life-sustaining procedures withheld or withdrawn and to be able to delegate the execution of that decision to others.

The right to die is controversial, replete with ethical, moral, religious, and legal issues. You probably have some feeling about how you would like your situation to be handled if you had a terminal medical condition.

Many times, when a crucial medical issue arises, the person with the most at stake—the patient—is unable to communicate intelligently. By signing a health-care directive before incompetence becomes an issue, you are not relinquishing any immediate control. As long as you are able to direct the physician, you speak for yourself. If at some later point you are unable to communicate or are judged incompetent, you'll still have a hand in guiding family and health-care providers via your health-care directive.

It's possible that even without health-care directives, your family and physician will be able to navigate an acceptable course of action for your care if it becomes necessary. They might even make the same choices you would. However, without health-care directives, it is less likely that your wishes will be followed. Unique circumstances, the personalities of family members, or the philosophy of the physician or even a hospital administrator can become a factor in what are literally life-and-death matters. When this happens, your fate is in question, and your family is dragged through what can be an extremely painful and expensive process that can take on a life of its own.

The Patient Self-Determination Act requires hospitals, nursing homes, and other medical institutions that receive federal funding to inform patients of their right to execute health-care directives. However, there is no law requiring patients to follow through. It's still up to you to get it done.

Power of Attorney for Health Care

A power of attorney for health care is generally more important than a living Will. It is provided for by statute in most states and may be referred to as a Statutory Short Form Power of Attorney for Health Care. This document allows you to express your philosophy regarding life-sustaining procedures and lets you appoint an agent (also called a "proxy" or a "surrogate") to make your health-care decisions for you when you are unable to do so.

Your agent can be any competent adult except, in most states, your own treating physician. If a relative of yours happens to be a physician but is not your personal physician, you can choose that person as your agent.

Generally speaking, the best choices are close and trusted loved ones, particularly if they live nearby. You should name a primary agent and, in case that person is unable to act, additional agents listed consecutively in the document. Selecting an agent can be a difficult decision, but it's better to make a tough or imperfect choice than to do nothing.

FUN FACT

In some states, if you select your spouse as your health-care agent and later get divorced, their appointment is considered automatically revoked unless it is renewed after the divorce. The legislature figures that nobody wants an ex-spouse empowered to come running into the hospital to "pull the plug" or prolong an ex's agonizing existence.

You can make a power of attorney for health care effective immediately or at some time in the future, such as when your treating physician says that you cannot effectively communicate regarding health decisions. Don't worry that you're signing away your free will; as long as you, the principal, can articulate your wishes regarding health-care decisions, you still have unquestioned authority over your own medical care.

You can direct your agent to act on your behalf in any manner you choose. The Illinois Statutory Power of Attorney for Health Care offers two statements of philosophy about life-sustaining treatment from which to choose. These statements, listed below, can be used as templates, or you can write something of your own design:

1. The quality of my life is more important than the length of my life. If I am unconscious and my attending physician believes, in accordance with reasonable medical standards, that I will not wake up or recover my ability to think, communicate with my family and friends, and experience my surroundings, I do not want treatments to prolong my life or delay my death, but I do want treatment or care to make me comfortable and to relieve me of pain.

2. Staying alive is more important to me, no matter how sick I am, how much I am suffering, the cost of the procedures, or how unlikely my chances for recovery are. I want my life to be prolonged to the greatest extent possible in accordance with reasonable medical standards.

Unless specifically limited, most statutory powers of attorney for health care give your agent the authority to make any decision regarding your medical care you would be able to make if capable of communicating your wishes.

A power of attorney for health care can grant authority to withhold nutrients and hydration (food and water). If you do not want to be left in a diminished capacity, unable to communicate, with no hope of recovery, instructions to withhold food and water, in a humane manner, might be the only way to have your wishes granted.

Your agent's authority can be limited in any fashion you wish, including but not limited to the listing of any medical procedures that you find abhorrent. You may insist on:

- No electrical or mechanical resuscitation of the heart when it has stopped beating;
- No nasogastric (feeding-tube) feeding when paralyzed or unable to take nourishment by mouth; or
- No mechanical respiration when unable to sustain breathing.

You may place limits on the power to make an anatomical gift, authorize an autopsy, and also specify when to attempt to resuscitate or not take such measures.

Though most people associate the power of attorney for health care with the metaphorical "pull the plug" decision, in the event of incapacity, it gives your agent decision-making authority over other personal items, such as where you live (nursing home versus your own home with an appropriate level of caregiving), along with treatment A versus treatment B.

In order to properly execute a power of attorney for health care, you must sign the document in the presence of at least one witness who is neither an heir nor your treating physician.

A WORD OF ADVICE

With regard to Wills, powers of attorney, Trusts, and living Wills, some states require a second witness and/or a notary's seal. I suggest two witnesses and a notary for all of these documents, even if such execution requirements are not mandated by the state in which you reside.

After you have executed the power of attorney for health care, you may want to give copies of it to your physician and others associated with your health care, such as a nursing home or another facility. Ask them to make it a permanent part of your medical file. This way, even if your family cannot find a copy of the document in an emergency, your medical provider will have it on hand.

Surrogate Acts

Many states, including Illinois, have what are known as Surrogate Acts, which apply in the event of a terminal illness or a hopeless condition. These Surrogate Acts direct that if you have not executed a power of attorney for health care, your health-care provider can select a person to act as agent on your behalf, in the event that you become unable to speak for yourself. Even if this is invoked, you may be better off making the selection of an agent yourself. Just as a court can pick a health-care agent contrary to your wishes, so can the health-care provider, and if there is a family dispute, the hospital will avoid making any decision that can lead to it being named as party to a lawsuit.

Without a power of attorney for health care, the "wrong" person is particularly likely to be selected to speak for you if:

- You have a longtime significant other to whom you are not legally married;
- You are married but are separated or otherwise not on good terms with your spouse;
- You have at least one child who does not know of your wishes;
- Your parents are still alive, but you have not discussed the matter with them;
- You are married but have children from a previous marriage, especially if they don't have a good relationship with your new spouse or have philosophical differences with him or her over matters relating to your health care;
- Your closest relatives have religious or other philosophical views you do not share regarding life-and-death decisions; or
- You have no close family.

REAL-LIFE STORIES

Phil had a twenty-five-year relationship with a partner to whom he was not married. Phil became incapacitated with a serious medical condition that rendered him unable to communicate. Phil's family did not approve of his lifestyle and excluded his partner from all decision making, instead taking charge themselves, although the

REAL-LIFE STORIES

family had been estranged from him, and they had not even spoken for years.

Straight, gay, bi, or q, if you are in a long-standing relationship lacking the formality of marriage, you must realize that your main companion(s) have no legal standing to make decisions on your behalf. For those who plan ahead, however, this problem is easily overcome.

Sometimes people learn the importance of a power of attorney for health care the hard way. Vivian had to undergo a serious surgical procedure. When she awoke in the hospital after the operation, she was given some bad news: While the operation had been a success, a second operation would be necessary. The surgeons had discovered an additional condition during the first operation, but without Vivian's consent, they were not legally able to address that problem. Even a successful procedure could have conceivably led to a lawsuit. An agent under a power of attorney for health care could have provided that consent and saved Vivian from a second surgery. Before the second procedure, Vivian put a power of attorney for health care in place, selecting an agent who could make decisions during the time that she couldn't.

The Living Will

Almost every state has a living Will statute that allows an individual, officially known as the declarant, to state that they do not wish to be kept alive by extraordinary medical procedures.

While the power of attorney for health care is an action document that relates to any medical decision, the living Will is a static document describing your philosophy regarding metaphorical "pull-the-plug" decisions. A living Will is less effective than a power of attorney for health care; moreover, the power of attorney for health care takes precedence over a living Will whenever the agent named in the power is available.

If, after signing a living Will, you become unable to communicate due to an accident or illness, the living Will speaks for you. The physician is then authorized by the document itself to withhold or withdraw life-sustaining procedures within a limited set of circumstances without risk of incurring liability for that act.

The living Will becomes effective only in a very specific situation: when the declarant is unable to communicate and has a terminal condition. In such a case, the physician is instructed not to provide care that will only delay dying. Care that serves another purpose, such as reducing pain or offering a possible cure, can still be administered.

An Example of a Living Will

The relevant portions of a typical state living Will statute read:

"I, Janet Doe, being of sound mind, willfully and voluntarily make known my desire that my moment of death shall not be artificially postponed under the circumstances set forth below, and do hereby declare:

"If at any time I should have an incurable and irreversible injury, disease, or illness judged to be a terminal condition by my attending physician, who has personally examined me and has determined that my death is imminent except for death-delaying procedures, I direct that such procedures that would only prolong the dying process be withheld or withdrawn, and that I be permitted to die naturally with only the administration of medication, sustenance, or the performance of any medical procedure deemed necessary by my attending physician to provide me with comfort care.

"In addition, I direct that such death-delaying procedures be withheld or withdrawn if there is no reasonable expectation of my recovery from physical or mental disability. I ask that drugs be mercifully administered to me for terminal suffering, even if they hasten the moment of my death.

"In the absence of my ability to give directions regarding the use of such death-delaying procedures, it is my intention that this declaration shall be honored by my family and physician as the final expression of my legal right to refuse medical or surgical treatment and accept the consequences from such refusal."

Since the living Will is simply a statement of philosophy, you may modify it with any language that you feel more accurately reflects your own thoughts. You might use different philosophical guidelines and instructions. Refer to some of the suggestions I listed in the previous power of attorney for health care pages to give you an idea on where you might draw the line regarding various medical procedures.

The problem with adding details is that it's almost impossible to prepare for every contingency. Rather than attempting to list every last situation in a living Will, make your power of attorney for health care as detailed as you wish and trust your agent to cover unforeseen occurrences.

The way I look at it, the main purpose of the living Will is to give cover to the agent under a power of attorney for health care to make the metaphorical "pull-the-plug" decision ("it's what Dad wants, he even says it in writing") and also give direction to the medical provider in the event that there is no agent under a power of attorney willing and able to make a decision regarding the end-of-life decision.

REAL-LIFE STORIES

Two grown sisters, Sally, 34, and Jennifer, 32, were informed that their father, Paul, 71, was in a coma in a Chicago-area hospital. Jennifer had cared for him the previous ten years and knew his philosophy regarding being kept alive when he had been suffering from an extremely poor quality of life for too long. Paul had made it a point to discuss the matter with Jennifer because he had been in failing health for years. However, he had delayed making his wishes official through the proper estate-planning documents.

Per Paul's earlier request, Jennifer asked to have her father's life support disconnected. Sally did not agree. She had had little to do with her father's care, having moved to Oregon years earlier, but she visited when Paul entered the hospital.

Sally insisted that Paul's life support be maintained. Perhaps she felt guilty about the fact that she'd been away so long. Perhaps her personal philosophy was that any human life should always be maintained. Perhaps it was a matter of sibling rivalry, and as the older sister, she wanted to keep the dominance she had had when both were children. Whatever the reason, Paul's failure to document his personal philosophy and to choose a health-care agent between his daughters created family strife and prolonged his life against his wishes, while his savings were depleted by hospital bills and legal costs from the guardianship battle.

HOW TO DEFEAT PROCRASTINATION

If you're procrastinating out of fear, you can help eliminate the fear by getting more information.

As you make decisions about what you need to do to get your affairs in order, what's missing, and how to handle the task, your fear will decrease, and you will be able to get started.

Do-Not-Resuscitate Orders (DNRs)

Unfortunately, health-care directives are not always honored by hospitals, physicians, or paramedics. The final document needed to prevent unwanted last-minute medical heroics is a DNR, or "Do Not Resuscitate" order, withholding CPR (cardiopulmonary resuscitation) and other "heroics," which is signed by an attending physician on request from a patient or the patient's designated health-care agent. DNRs are very common in intensive-care wards and are the final word on life-sustaining treatment. If a DNR has been issued, it should be posted prominently near the patient's bed or in her home.

POLST (Physician Orders for Life-Sustaining Treatment) forms and other similar acronyms that bear close resemblance to DNRs often list various treatments beyond CPR that the patient desires or finds abhorrent.

Organ Donation

Many states actively promote programs where drivers indicate consent on the backs of their driver's licenses to make anatomical gifts, under whatever restrictions the drivers wish to impose.

A power of attorney for health care is another critical place to state your intentions regarding organ donation or authorizing any other means of anatomical gifts. In fact, many of the statutory powers of attorney for health care forms contain a section devoted to this subject, where you can permit your agent to donate any organ or specify certain organs for donation. To ensure that your intentions are followed, you should have your preferences for organ donation explained on both your driver's license and your health-care power of attorney. In addition, you should make your wishes known to your family.

For those who have not given the matter much thought, consider that many thousands of people suffer needlessly or even die each year for lack of donor organs. Especially needed are young donors because their organs tend to be more robust. Unfortunately, many young people don't bother with organ-donor arrangements since they feel that death is so distant. But accidents happen. Through organ donation, even a senseless death might come to have some meaning.

For elderly persons who feel that "nobody will want my organs anyway," that can be a false belief if they agree that organs and tissues may be used for research and education, perhaps not helping anyone directly but enhancing knowledge to help many.

Avoid Guardianship of the Estate with a Power of Attorney for Property

Failure to plan for the possibility of becoming temporarily or permanently unable to handle your own finances can lead to another type of living probate known as guardianship of the estate. As with guardianship of the person, guardianship of the estate requires your family to go through a court proceeding to appoint a guardian to act on your behalf to handle such tasks as signing checks.

The best way to avoid guardianship over your estate is to execute a durable power of attorney for property while you are still competent to make your own decisions, appointing an agent to perform financial transactions on your behalf. It's "durable" because it survives incapacity.

Perhaps as a reflection of our aging population, probate courts today are crowded with people seeking the appointment of guardians to perform financial transactions for older, incompetent individuals. As a result, legislatures throughout the country have enacted statutes providing for a durable power of attorney for property in order to avoid such court proceedings.

The document is relatively simple; it allows you to select a trusted agent to handle your financial transactions during any period of your disability or incompetence without the necessity of petitioning the probate court for formal guardianship of your estate.

This can be a vital tool if you become incapacitated and you need someone to handle necessary or time-sensitive financial transactions. Even if you already have a Trust with a named successor trustee, you should have a durable power of attorney for property as well because a trustee is able to handle only transactions involving assets that are in the Trust. For example, you might need someone to:

- Transfer an asset from your personal estate into a Trust,
- Act on your behalf with respect to a joint tenancy asset,
- Go into your safe-deposit box,
- Sign and file your tax return,
- Pay your rent or mortgage,
- Pay insurance premiums or make a claim,
- Renew a certificate of deposit that has matured in your IRA,
- Make gifts to family members, or
- Sign a nursing home or other contract.

The durable power of attorney for property grants your agent the power to act within the parameters that you create. In most states, you can choose whether the document becomes effective when it's signed or at some future date, such as when your primary physician determines, in writing, and following a personal examination, that you are unable to manage your financial transactions.

In most states, the durable power of attorney for property also can end at any time you dictate, such as when you regain your capacity, but it always ends upon your death. A delicate dance is required to make sure the durable power of attorney for property is usable when it is needed but not subject to abuse prior to or even after it is needed.

Here is an example of language that demonstrates your desire for your family to act under a power of attorney for property on your behalf, but only at some time in the future (and in states that allow such springing language—Florida not being one of those states): "This power of attorney shall become effective when my spouse, living and competent (or if my spouse is not living or not competent, when a majority of my children who are living and competent), certifies in writing along with my attending physician, who has personally examined me, that in their judgment I am unable properly to manage my financial affairs."

For any power of attorney to be official, you must sign (or "mark") it while you are competent. In most states, one or two witnesses must attest to your signature in the presence of a notary public, who must also "notarize" the document. Only an original power of attorney, as opposed to a photocopy, can be used to transfer real estate.

Durable versus Nondurable Power of Attorney

A nondurable power of attorney is designed to serve a specific purpose and then end. It also automatically ends if you die or become incompetent. A nondurable power of attorney may be general or limited. A general power of attorney may be used when one party is representing another in negotiations. A limited power of attorney is most often used for a specific transaction, such as when you are unable to be physically present to sign documents or handle a certain transaction. For example, if you are party to a real estate closing and are unable to be present at the closing, you can give someone a limited power of attorney, which is effective for a set period of time and relates only to that transaction. If the principal of a nondurable general or limited power of attorney becomes incompetent, the agent's authority ends.

A durable power of attorney, conversely, is called "durable" because it survives any subsequent disability or incompetence. It was created to enable you to plan for such a possibility.

Differences between a durable power of attorney and a nondurable power of attorney (whether general or limited):

Durable Power of Attorney	Nondurable Power of Attorney
Its purpose is to allow a person to act on your behalf with respect to any financial transaction that is in your interest (only upon incapacity, if "springing").	Its purpose is to allow a person to act on your behalf with respect to some specific financial transaction or series of transactions.
It survives subsequent incapacity.	It relates only to a specific transaction or series of transactions.
It applies with respect to a very wide range of transactions under the parameters you set.	It ends upon subsequent incapacity.
It's effective either when it's signed or at some future date or triggering (springing) event, such as when selected parties determine you are unable to conduct business transactions.	It's usually limited for a set period of time and until the specific transaction or transactions are completed, or is ongoing based on various business factors.
It ends at any time you dictate and, if springing, when you regain your ability to conduct business transactions.	It ends at any time you dictate, usually when a specific transaction is completed or a business relationship changes.

All powers of attorney, whether durable or not, must be signed by you in the presence of a notary, while you are competent. Requirement of an independent witness varies from state to state, but the best practice for execution is having two non-related witnesses in addition to the notarization.

All financial powers of attorney, whether they are durable or general, terminate upon your death.

Another useful tool in avoiding guardianship over your estate is establishing and fully funding a revocable living Trust (also called a revocable Trust, chapter 8). ●

Action Plan Five: Don't Stop Now!

A six-step strategy to prepare for your own incapacity:

1. Today, take a moment to consider how you would like your health care to be handled if you are ever severely injured, your chances for recovery are slim, and you are unable to communicate. Put your thoughts into writing.

2. If your thoughts on these matters are not clear, speak to people you trust. Ask your doctor for advice, or ask people you know who have lived through brutal illnesses or injuries and gone through extensive medical procedures.

3. During the next week, decide who would best represent your health-care interests if you were incapacitated. Is there a close friend or relative whose judgment you trust? Is this person likely to be available when needed? Discuss with your prospective agent your philosophy on sustaining or ending your life if you are in a hopeless medical condition. Would they be willing to act according to your wishes?

4. If you have special circumstances, such as a divisive relationship among your relatives, plan to minimize any potential disharmony. One example is when there is bad blood between your current spouse and your grown children from a previous marriage. If you believe that there may be conflict regarding your care, it is important to be very specific about delegating the proper authority to be exercised under certain conditions.

5. Take a look at your own state's living Will statute, and search for your own voice about a philosophy reflective of your belief regarding how you would want your imminent death handled within the context of a terminal illness or injury. Put your thoughts on paper, and show an attorney at a meeting.

6. Relax; take a break. You have made terrific progress in completing your estate-planning goals!

CHAPTER 6

Protecting Your Assets While You're Around to Enjoy Them

"I'm not dead (yet)."
—Unfortunate peasant protesting that he is not ready to be carted away, in Monty Python and the Holy Grail

Estate planning can help you protect your estate from those who would like to grab it from you. However, there are many nuances involved in sufficiently armoring yourself. As a result, there are whole books devoted to this topic, so if you are losing sleep at night worrying about your liabilities, read this chapter and then go buy a more specialized treatment of the subject.

The Threat of Lawsuits

Suing people long ago replaced baseball as our national pastime. Many people lose sleep over the threat of a lawsuit—and many of those who don't *would* if they realized how little it would take for them to lose everything they own.

Members of professions that are at particularly high risk for lawsuits, such as physicians or, ironically, lawyers, have additional reason to be obsessed with potential liabilities, although every American is a potential victim. Are the lawyers to blame for the explosion of lawsuits? Certainly, the contingency-fee arrangement, in which an attorney is paid a percentage of the amount collected (often 33% or more), is a factor.

But lawyers can also be a solution—estate-planning lawyers, anyway, because it is possible to protect yourself through estate planning. Lawsuit protection (also commonly referred to as asset protection) has a place in this book only because the tools often used are estate-planning tools and can be arranged by estate-planning lawyers. But protecting your assets during your life is also a way to ensure that they'll be there after your death, for your heirs.

Let's say you are driving late at night and hit another car from behind. You exchange insurance information and learn the following week that the other person (the plaintiff) has hired a lawyer. The plaintiff claims to have suffered a personal injury. You have auto insurance, but the plaintiff asks for more money than your insurance policy limits (the maximum amount your insurance company can be obligated to pay).

If the lawsuit results in a judgment greater than the amount your insurance will cover, that makes it a subject for estate planning. This isn't too unusual; juries are often more than willing to throw around other people's money like confetti.

At this point, the plaintiff may go after your personal assets. First, depending on the size of the judgment, virtually all of your assets could be seized or have liens placed on them—liens that must be satisfied before you can pocket any money when the assets are sold. Next, if the plaintiff's damages still are not paid, your future earnings could be garnished (a portion of your paycheck goes to someone else). While the plaintiff sues the manufacturer of the car they're driving or the city where the accident happened, you can be cleaned out.

Assessing Your Risk of Losing Assets in a Lawsuit

Not everyone has the same risk of losing his or her assets in a lawsuit. High-risk groups include, but are not limited to:

- Physicians, lawyers, and certain small-business owners.
- People with minimal liability coverage on their auto or homeowner's insurance.
- Those who own assets together with other people. For example, if you own your house in joint tenancy (discussed in more detail in chapter 8), you could lose it if the other joint owner is successfully sued. Partnership and corporate assets can also be lost to a plaintiff's claim against your partner or corporate associate or because of the negligence of your partner or an employee.
- The rich and famous, who make appealing targets for lawsuits, frivolous and otherwise.

HOW TO DEFEAT PROCRASTINATION

If you're just not in the mood, ask yourself, "Is there anything—any part of this task—I'd be willing to do right now?"

If the answer is "no," find an activity, anything, and do it, then get back to the question above. The activity doesn't even have to be related to the task. Sometimes, you just need to get your motor running. Once you're busy, you'll find it's often easier to switch gears and get to the important task at hand than if you are just thinking about doing something without making progress.

Protecting Personal Assets

Protecting personal assets from lawsuits is a complex subject, and certainly anyone with an extremely large estate to protect or with some other reason to believe they are likely to be the victim of a lawsuit might decide to consult a specialist.

Here are a few simple strategies to minimize your risk.

Strategy 1: Buy Liability and Umbrella Insurance

Almost everyone with a house or a car has homeowner's and automobile insurance policies. If you have a mortgage on your house, your lender will mandate homeowner's insurance. Auto liability insurance is required of drivers in most states. But those who rent their homes are often lax about purchasing renter's insurance, typically a low-cost form of insurance that can protect against both lawsuits and theft.

Many people fail to take advantage of umbrella coverage. Umbrella policies can be extremely useful in filling in gaps in other insurance policies when it comes to liability. For just a few hundred dollars a year or less, you can add millions of dollars of liability protection to your existing coverage. If you don't have an umbrella policy, ask your home and auto insurance providers if it's something they offer. If you have a job that carries the risk of a lawsuit, you also need professional liability or errors-and-omissions insurance, and if you own a small business, you may need more insurance to protect you from various potential liabilities.

Strategy 2: Incorporation

Forming a corporation is a common and effective method of protecting personal assets from business-related liabilities. But incorporating should not be viewed as the ultimate protection. The shield that the corporation offers from personal liability can be defeated. This is commonly referred to by lawyers as "piercing the corporate veil."

How can this happen? If you incorporate, your personal assets should be protected from acts of negligence by your employees, but what if you are personally negligent? The law mandates that a corporation and its principals comply with many different rules and regulations, so it can be easy to unintentionally violate one of these rules or regulations.

Under many circumstances, your personal assets can be used to satisfy an outstanding corporate liability. Even if an employee other than yourself acted negligently, all kinds of theories can be bootstrapped to lay the ultimate negligence at your personal doorstep.

Strategy 3: Forming a Limited Partnership or a Limited Liability Company

Forming a limited partnership (LP) or a limited liability company (LLC) is also a common and effective method of protecting personal assets from various types of liabilities. Let's say that you own a building and are afraid that people might injure themselves on the premises. Creditors of a limited partner or a member of an LLC generally cannot reach LP or LLC assets or force their way into the LP or LLC business. While a creditor might be able to obtain the right to receive a partner's or a member's share of distributions from the LP or the LLC, if the entity makes no distributions, the assets are protected from his creditors.

LPs and LLCs can function as handy asset-protection tools while serving various estate-planning needs as well. More on LPs and LLCs in chapter 12.

Revocable Trusts and Prenuptial Agreements

Revocable Trusts can be used to help protect your assets in case of a divorce. Let's say you're a reasonably successful person about to get married. Do you ask your spouse-to-be for a prenuptial agreement?

Most people cringe at the thought of raising the topic and putting the nascent relationship at risk, but what about the possibility of losing half your assets? Revocable Trusts can provide a partial solution, helping ensure that your assets will remain your assets in the event of a divorce.

Before you wed, all of your major personal assets are placed into the Trust. Precise bookkeeping is crucial to doing this correctly. These Trust assets, which you accumulated prior to marriage, must be kept segregated from those you acquire after the marriage. Assets that are mixed with those of your newly beloved are at increased risk in a divorce. Assets can be removed from your pre-established Trust if you so choose, but after the wedding, new assets cannot be moved into it.

This is not a foolproof method for protecting assets—in truth, neither is a prenuptial agreement—but it's a solid tool.

It's also less inflammatory than a prenuptial agreement because:

- You don't have to get a signature from your future spouse; you don't even have to mention that you have a Trust or that assets have been transferred to it;
- You avoid the use of the hot-button term *prenup*, which carries all sorts of baggage with it; and
- You can avoid disclosing to your spouse all of your assets, something that is required for a valid prenuptial. ●

Action Plan Six: You're Getting There!

A five-step plan to reduce risks to your estate:
1. Today, consider your risk of liability. Is there any particular reason to believe you could become the target of a lawsuit? Are you in an occupation in which you may be sued because of your work?

Action Plan Six: You're Getting There!

3. Within the next week, discuss your liability coverage with your insurance agent, and, if appropriate, plug the gaps. Do you have umbrella insurance?
4. Review the estate-planning tools that might offer you some lawsuit protection and discuss them with your attorney.
5. If you are planning to get married, think about the possibility of divorce. Hopefully, you aren't going into marriage expecting to get divorced, but it doesn't hurt to take steps to protect your assets. Improper planning may result in your losing substantially more assets in a divorce than would otherwise be the case. If you are really on the fence about whether to get married because of financial concerns, don't.

CHAPTER 7

The Cost of Death Probate and Ways to Avoid It

"Being of sound mind, I spent it all."
—Leon Jaworski, referring to the shortest Will on record

Do you care about your family? If you fail to properly plan your estate, it's your family who suffers. Incomplete or poor planning leads to considerable delays, sizable legal costs, and taxes, too. It's possible to protect your family from the worst of these, but doing so requires proper utilization of the estate-planning tools at your disposal.

Some of the concepts involved in this process can be a bit complex or, at least, unpleasant to think about. But remember, that's why you're working with an estate-planning attorney. The message of this chapter is straightforward: Use Trusts. For those wanting to look after their families, Trusts of various shapes and sizes will play a key role. But before we get to Trusts, we'll consider what may happen with your estate if you fail to prepare properly.

Death Probate

We've already discussed two forms of living probate—guardianships of the estate and guardianships of the person, often avoidable through the use of durable powers of attorney for property and health care.

In this chapter, we turn to death probate, the more familiar form of probate that occurs at death. Death probate is not a punishment that the government dreamed up to inflict on grieving families, even if it does sometimes seem that way. The probate court was established under British common law to provide a mechanism for beneficiaries to obtain clear and absolute ownership of an asset after the previous owner has died. It is, in effect, a lawsuit brought by heirs against potential creditors and other claimants, naming the person or the entity that controls the administration process (the executor) and eventually cutting off any claims, so that title to assets is clear, and no future claims will be recognized.

In simple terms, it is the connection between the dead person's assets and the beneficiaries who receive those assets.

Before title to an asset can be transferred to an heir, the probate court must ensure that all bills and claims against the deceased's estate are paid and that other safeguards are taken to ensure that the assets are transferred to the correct beneficiaries.

The executor of the estate (the "administrator," if the individual died without a Will; either term is also referred to as the "personal representative") gathers the assets of the testator (the deceased person), pays any debts and taxes, notifies heirs, and eventually distributes whatever is left to the beneficiaries, per your directions if you left a Will or the laws of intestate succession if you didn't. Probate rules vary from state to state, but all require that assets remain in the estate for some minimum period of time, often around six months, so that any creditors have time to assert their claims against those assets.

Since probate involves going to court—that is, a public forum in which lawsuits are brought—it tends to increase the chances that your estate plan will be contested.

Typical issues in Will contests include:

- The competency of the deceased when the Will was signed,

- Improper execution of the Will,
- Duress or undue influence by another person, and
- Inadequate consideration to a surviving spouse (see chapter 11).

If a Will is contested, the drain of assets from legal fees and other expenses from the estate can be enormous. Your risk can be reduced greatly through the use of a revocable Trust, covered in chapter 8. In most states, revocable Trusts are signed with much less formality than Wills, and they're less likely to be subject to attack on technical grounds.

FUN FACT—OR FICTION?

The word *testator*, like *testify*, derives from the same root as *testicle*. In Roman times, oaths were sworn while gripping one's "family jewels."

Part of the probate court's function is determining which person shall act as guardian for any minor children and selecting your personal representative, who is the executor or the administrator collecting your assets, paying your debts, and distributing your remaining assets. If your children are minors, guardianship will have to be established in a separate probate proceeding, with yearly accountings submitted for court approval and a surety bond to be paid every year until they reach the age of majority, usually 18 or 21. At that time, if there is no Trust, they will get their entire remaining inheritance, all at once, with no strings attached—party time!

The Cost of Probate

Most families hire a lawyer to probate an estate. The lawyer may charge an hourly fee, a flat fee, a percentage fee based on the size of the estate, or some combination of the above. In addition, there will be assorted court costs and related fees. Note that your family is under no obligation to hire the attorney who drafted your Will just because the attorney keeps the original document in his vault.

It's difficult to give a precise figure for the cost of probate, as it varies based on the size of the estate and how long the process takes, which in some cases can be years. It also varies greatly from state to state. In some states, there are statutes regulating attorney fees in probate proceedings. An often-mentioned rule-of-thumb figure is that the probate process will deplete 2 to 10 percent of the value of the estate. If the estate is contested, then the cost is anyone's guess.

If your estate must be probated, the cost will most likely be considerably more than you would have paid an estate-planning attorney to design an estate plan that could have bypassed the process. If your failure to plan is driven by thriftiness, it's likely you're being penny wise and pound foolish. Besides, the dollar cost doesn't reflect the time, inconvenience, anguish, and humiliation that the probate process can cause the family.

Adding to the potential cost of death, a probate estate must be opened in every state where you own real estate. For example, if a New York resident dies owning a condominium in Florida, the executor must hire a separate attorney in Florida to open up an ancillary probate estate because New York courts have no jurisdiction over the Florida property.

Passing your assets to your heirs through the probate process is often the least convenient, most expensive option available. Yet probate is the option that many people unintentionally choose for their family, simply by failing to take the necessary steps to avoid it. A Will alone will not avoid probate over your assets.

Probate Fees

California's probate fees, including attorneys' and executors' fees, are based on gross estate assets before any reduction for debts (for example, the total value of your house, rather than your equity in it). The fees, which are probably about average for the fifty states, are set by statute in California, though the attorney and the executor may charge less. These fees do not include filing costs and bond premiums; nor do they include appraisal and other special fees that may be involved in the sale of assets or the fees charged for tax preparation, which would be paid regardless of whether there is probate. In addition, if there are other complicating factors, such as a Will challenge, the court may approve higher attorney and executor fees.

Value of Estate	Rate
Up to $100,000	4%
Next $100,000	3%
Next $800,000	2%
Next $9 million	1%
Next $15 million	0.5%
Over $25 million	A reasonable fee to be determined by the court.

Source: California probate code.

If the executor and the attorney *each* receive the statutory fee, you can double the amount noted above. In many states, attorneys and executors are simply entitled to "reasonable compensation." If it takes years to close an estate, the attorneys can take a huge slice—and given this fact, they may appear to be dragging their feet, though that is neither ethical nor embraced by the court.

The Advantages of Probate

Although estate-planning professionals often advocate the use of revocable living Trusts to avoid probate, sometimes administering an estate via probate is better than avoiding it.

Three reasons that probate can be advantageous:

- Creditors' claims can be cut off more quickly using a probate proceeding than if assets are passed through a Trust. Claims on a probate estate must be made within a certain time period—usually six to twelve months, depending on the state—provided proper notice of death is given. After that period of time, all creditor claims are cut off. In contrast, creditors' claims against a Trust are treated like claims against the deceased as an individual. Often, this means that claims can be pressed well beyond a six-to-twelve-month time frame. When there are potential creditors, some people choose to negate this problem through a simple probate conducted on nominal assets. It works like this: The vast majority of the estate is in the Trust, but some small amount, say $10, is put through probate for the sole purpose of eliminating claims on the entire estate once the probate period ends. Even though only a small amount of money passed through probate, this may eliminate claims on the entire estate, provided proper notification is made to creditors.

- You trust your trustee only to a certain extent. If you select a trustee who is a closet embezzler, the Trust could get wiped out before anyone has a chance to discover what's been done. While this book often advocates the privacy afforded by funded revocable living Trusts, it must be acknowledged that sometimes there is an advantage in having the probate court keep an eye on things. Selecting a bank trustee (also discussed in the next chapter) may ease your mind with regard to the possibility of a bad trustee looting or otherwise completely undermining the purpose of a Trust.

- With a probate estate you have the choice of either a calendar or a fiscal year income-tax-year election. With a Trust, if there is no associated probate, the calendar year must be used. Why is this a problem? For ninety-nine people out of one hundred it isn't, but sometimes using a fiscal year election may delay a tax filing deadline or even result in lower taxes.

REAL-LIFE STORIES

The author's own estate plan is a good example of an intentional probate: My profession, estate-planning law, is one where there is theoretically no end to the threat of liability. If the heirs of one of my clients decide to try to sue me even after my death, perhaps thinking that I'd made some costly mistake in their parents' estate plan, they might be able to move forward with a case. That's why I've arranged to have a pro forma probate proceeding done on minimal assets after my death, even though substantially all of my assets are held in Trust. Anything is possible, and I sleep better knowing that some lawsuit won't pop up and devastate my heirs many years after I'm gone and unable to defend myself.

Simplified Probate—Independent Administration

Many states have reformed their probate codes to allow a simplified probate known as independent administration. This allows a Will to be probated with virtually no supervision from the probate court, and it can significantly lower probate costs.

If all of the creditors and the beneficiaries go along with this simplified process, the probate can be accomplished with as few as two court appearances, one opening the estate and one closing it. In between, the executor can collect, inventory, and administer the estate and pay debts without constantly checking in with the probate judge.

If a creditor or a beneficiary becomes disenchanted with the executor, that party may object to the independent administration, and the estate may be put into a regular supervised probate, resulting in more court involvement and thereby higher attorney fees.

Loss of Privacy in Probate

Probate is a public process. Anyone can examine your probate court file, including your Will, if you have one, because it must be filed as a public document. In addition, a notice of your death must be filed in a local newspaper so that any creditors unknown to the executor can initiate claims. In the absence of probate, there is no requirement to publish a notice, although if there is a Will, that must still be filed in the court. However, if the Will is a "pour-over Will" (chapter 9), the information that can be gleaned from it is minimal.

In probate, all of the assets passing through the estate are inventoried in the court file. Anyone can attend the probate hearings and examine the court files, as they are open to the general public. If this doesn't bother you, perhaps it should. Do you want just anyone to have access to information about your beneficiaries, including their contact information and the gifts they receive from your estate?

Probate without a Will

When a person dies intestate—that is, without a Will—probate costs can be particularly high. For example, in Cook County, Illinois (Chicago and suburbs), in addition to the attorneys' and the executors' fees, the usual probate filing fee is about $500, plus publishing a notice to unknown heirs costs about $250. Also, a surety bond, often waived in a Will, must be paid yearly on an intestate estate until the estate is closed. The purpose of the surety bond is to compensate the estate if it is handled incorrectly and is based on the value of the estate, about $3,500 per year for a million-dollar estate.

Attorneys' fees, always a consideration, generally run higher for intestate estates than for an uncontested Will because the attorney might have to:

- Spend more time with the decedent's family determining the proper heirs;
- Spend more time in front of the court proving who the rightful heirs are under the law; or
- Make a case for selecting the guardian of minor children without written input from the decedent, which can be a mess if there is no agreement among the family.

HOW TO DEFEAT PROCRASTINATION

Get help from someone. There is no rule that you must do everything yourself.

Intestacy

Beyond the probate fees incurred in an intestate estate, dying without a Will creates a few other problems.

The probate court determines who gets your assets, when, and in what percentages, according to the preset laws of intestacy, which vary from state to state. The intestate distribution system is designed to be fair, and it might work for your family, but often things don't work out exactly as you would desire. An Internet search for "(state of probate administration, where you primarily live and own real estate) intestate law" will give you an idea of who gets your probate assets if you die without a will.

Spouses and children generally share in intestate estates, and for beneficiaries other than spouses, the formulas generally favor *per stirpes* distributions. For instance, when referring to children, if there is a deceased child or other relation, then any share that that child or other relation would have received had the beneficiary survived will usually be distributed to that person's descendants, if any. Likewise, if a share is distributed to brothers and sisters, then any deceased brother's or sister's share will go to that sibling's descendants, your nieces and nephews (and great-nieces and -nephews if there are deceased nieces or nephews).

If there is no surviving spouse, descendants, parents, siblings, nephews, or nieces, then the laws of descent and distribution of the various states often extend to maternal and paternal grandparents or great-grandparents and their descendants, who are uncles, aunts, great-uncles and -aunts, and cousins of various degrees.

In a few states, if there is no surviving family whatsoever, the families of deceased spouses may be entitled to an intestate share. Also, in most, though not all, states, half-brothers and half-sisters are treated the same as full siblings, and that may also extend to other "half" relatives. In most instances, step relations (without adoptions) are not intestate beneficiaries.

If you have never been married and have no family descending from your grandparents or even great-grandparents, your estate may escheat—meaning it is transferred to the state in which you live, with real estate going to the county in which it is located.

REAL-LIFE STORIES

Gerald found out the hard way how the laws of intestacy can be inappropriate. His mother had died years earlier, and when his father died without a Will, the estate was divided evenly between Gerald and his brother, David. Sounds fair, right? Under normal circumstances, it

REAL-LIFE STORIES

would have been. But David had severe disabilities that left him eligible for government assistance when all his assets had been depleted. Thus, David's inheritance meant that he received less government assistance until the inheritance was completely used up. It was as if the government had inherited the money! Since Gerald provided his brother with everything that government programs do not, his father should have thought ahead and left David's money in a supplemental needs Trust with Gerald as trustee.

In the years since this happened, other techniques have become available to protect the receipt of government assistance, but they all involve jumping through a few hoops—namely, establishing a 1st party payback Trust (OBRA '93 (d)(4)(A) and transferring assets to it. Also, in many states, if there is a Trust, the assets can be "decanted" to a more restrictive Trust. Both of these actions involve much more time and money than setting up the right special needs Trust prior to death.

Probate with a Will

If you have a Will when you die, your assets will go, eventually, to the people or the charities that you name in your Will. Writing a Will also means that you nominate the guardian for your minor children. You also select the executor, along with the trustee for any testamentary Trusts, which are Trusts that become effective at your death (as opposed to living Trusts, which go into effect during your lifetime).

Other ways a Will can simplify the probate process:

- A Will can provide for a waiver of bond for the executor of your Will, which will reduce one aspect of the probate cost; and

- A Will can provide for independent administration by the executor as opposed to court-supervised administration, keeping court appearances to a minimum.

Selecting an Executor

The skills needed to be the executor of a Will are similar to those required to be a trustee of your Trust. Very often, the person selected to be trustee is named executor.

A major difference between the two roles is the potential duration of the time commitment. The trustee role can last for a long period of time because the job might go on for years, especially where minor children are involved or you want the trustee to control the assets on a discretionary basis. Hopefully, probate will not last for years, although under a nasty set of circumstances, it can.

Even with a Will, your executor will have to go to the county probate court and obtain a court order (usually called *letters of office* or *letters testamentary*) to get control of your assets. A Will, on its own, does not confer this authority. It simply tells the probate court where, when, and by whom your assets should be distributed upon your death.

The probate court establishes a Will's authenticity and officially appoints the executor named in the Will. Having a Will simplifies the probate proceeding because the court makes fewer choices regarding its administration. However, it does not eliminate the need for probate. Meanwhile, when your assets are being probated, it may be difficult for your heirs to gain access to them, a potential problem when loved ones need the funds in a hurry.

REAL-LIFE STORIES

Tim and Diane died together in an automobile accident four years ago, leaving three children, ages 16, 12, and

REAL-LIFE STORIES

11. They had done no estate planning, so their estate went into probate. The couple's estate was worth over $1 million—at least, until probate. Guardianship proceedings can be particularly expensive, and Tim's and Diane's families each argued that they should receive custody of the children. By the time the probate was over, more than $50,000 had been drained, and the children had spent half a year in limbo, uncertain where they would be living.

A year after that, Tim and Diane's oldest child, Jon, reached age 18 and inherited his share of their money. Without Trusts, all the money went into his hands on his birthday with no controls in place. Unfortunately, because the probate is a public process, an unscrupulous "salesman" knew the details of the inheritance and convinced Jon to put the lion's share of his money into a series of terrible investments. Jon's inheritance was ultimately insufficient to pay his way through college.

Transferring Property upon Death without Probate

If a Will isn't enough to avoid probate, what is? A number of different mechanisms can enable your beneficiary to take over your assets upon your death without probate. Some work better than others, depending on your situation.

1. Designating a beneficiary

   Certain assets, such as life insurance policies, annuities, and various retirement accounts, including IRAs and 401(k) s, typically allow you to designate a beneficiary to receive payment upon your death.

Banks, brokerages, and many mutual funds allow similar automatic transfers to a beneficiary upon your death. Such accounts may be called POD (Payable on Death) or TOD (Transfer on Death) accounts, and they allow such assets to be transferred without probate. This strategy is not available for all assets, however; most notably, it isn't always an option for real estate, though some states do allow for Transfer on Death Instruments (TODIs) that get filed with the appropriate state agency, and if you own the property at the time of your death, it is transferred according to the TODI. Moreover, a beneficiary designation might fail if the beneficiary dies before (or with) you and you failed to name a contingent beneficiary. If you rely exclusively on beneficiary designations as your estate plan, I highly suggest that you keep a confirmation *from* the financial institution as to all beneficiaries, including contingent ones, with either or both of your estate planning and financial files.

2. Joint tenancy with rights of survivorship

    You can name one or more persons as joint tenants of certain assets. A surviving joint tenant on the account will have access to the account after your death (and during your life—the person you select as a joint tenant thereafter has the same right to the account as you do; they could, for example, unilaterally withdraw all the money at any time).

    It might be more accurate to say that joint tenancy postpones probate, rather than avoids it. When the surviving joint tenant dies, the asset must then go through probate, unless the survivor has retitled the asset or added a new joint tenant. We'll cover various pluses and minuses of joint tenancy later in this chapter.

3. Assets held in Trust

    A revocable self-declaration of Trust is a simple and versatile way to transfer assets upon death. You fund the Trust by transferring the ownership of assets into the Trust during your lifetime. From that point, you no longer own the assets as an individual; you own them as the trustee of your Trust.

Upon your death, the assets in the Trust will be distributed according to the provisions of your Trust agreement.

4. Small estates

Small estates often can be transferred with an easy affidavit or some other simplified procedure to shortcut probate, as long as there are no unpaid creditors or disputes among the potential heirs. States vary in their definitions of a "small estate," but usually real estate cannot be dealt with via an affidavit.

5. Buy-sell agreement

A buy-sell agreement may be used to transfer a privately owned business such as a corporation or a partnership. In one typical structure, a life-insurance policy is purchased by the partnership for each partner. When one partner dies, the proceeds of the policy are used to buy out the interests of the deceased partner by paying an appropriate amount directly to his family, without probate. See chapter 12 for more details.

6. Tangible Personal property

Modest items of tangible personal property, such as clothing, furniture, and jewelry, usually can be divided among family members, without acrimony and without probate. Of course, sometimes the biggest family battles are over items with little market value but enormous sentimental value. Most estate plans deal with personal property in a cursory manner because listing all your "stuff" and deciding who gets what would be a time-consuming task—and you expect, or at least hope, that your beneficiaries will be fair in dealing with one another.

However, if you fear a family battle over tangible personal property, then take a look at some of my suggestions in chapter 12 about how to resolve a potentially difficult situation.

7. Land Trusts

Some states, notably Illinois, Arizona, and Florida, allow a bank or a Trust company to nominally own real estate in the form of a land Trust. Under this arrangement, the true owner's name is hidden from the public record and is named only in the bank/Trust company's internal records as a beneficiary.

This beneficial owner typically retains the power of direction to transfer the property and designates contingent beneficiaries who become the new beneficial owners upon his death. You have to pay the bank or the Trust company to establish and terminate a land Trust, along with annual fees.

Land Trusts do not protect the beneficial owner from liability arising out of accidents occurring on the subject property, nor do they allow the property to escape the reach of the beneficial owner's other creditors, but they do avoid probate if a beneficiary is effectively named in the land Trust agreement

Joint Tenancy with Rights of Survivorship: Not Always the Answer

Joint tenancy with rights of survivorship is a very popular way for two or more people to own an undivided interest in an asset. In some ways, joint tenancy's appeal is understandable: upon the death of one joint tenant, the other joint tenant (or tenants) automatically gains control of the entire asset.

Little, if any, paperwork is needed to handle the transfer of ownership. No question, it's easy to set up. Unfortunately, there may be potential problems, particularly when joint tenancy is used between two people who are not husband and wife, or when it's the exclusive planning device for a husband and a wife who would derive much greater benefits from a more thorough estate-planning process.

Joint Tenancy versus Tenancy in Common

A tenancy in common is not the same as a joint tenancy, although the two terms are sometimes confused. Under a joint tenancy, ownership is passed upon the death of one tenant to the other surviving joint tenant or tenants. Under a tenancy in common, ownership is transferred not to the surviving tenant or tenants, but to whomever the deceased tenant directs. Alternatively, ownership may go to the deceased's estate. The asset remains divided among the surviving original tenant and the new tenant(s) in common.

For example, suppose you own an apartment building in joint tenancy with your brother. When you die, the asset becomes his. But if you and your brother own the building through a tenancy in common, when you die, your brother still owns only his half, while your half is transferred to your estate or to whomever you designate in your Will or Trust.

Spousal Joint Tenancy

One of the most common uses of a joint tenancy is between husband and wife. Couples often settle on a joint tenancy of assets as a convenient way to avoid probate. Possessions held in joint tenancy do in fact avoid probate initially, but a close look illustrates some potential problems.

For example, consider a couple who owns their house in this manner. When the first spouse dies, the house will pass to the second without probate, as the couple had intended. Unless additional estate planning is done, however, the house will face probate when the second spouse dies. And if both spouses die at more or less the same time, probate will be required.

More important, joint tenancy can lead to estates being divided in ways that would not have met with the deceased's wishes. For example, if a widower with two children remarries and puts his property in joint tenancy with his new wife, his children will not inherit any of the joint tenancy assets when he dies—they go completely to the new wife.

This is not to say that spousal joint tenancy never makes sense. It's a perfectly viable option when used properly, but only when its limitations are understood and various consequences have been considered.

Non-Spousal Joint Tenancy

A joint tenancy between spouses might have a few complications, but larger problems develop when people use a joint tenancy between non-spouses. Often, such arrangements are made between a parent and an adult child. Even if disasters such as those discussed below don't occur, a joint tenancy can complicate the joint tenants' lives. To sell real estate held in joint tenancy, for example, all joint tenants must sign the deed or other necessary paperwork. This can, at worst, be a nightmare if the joint tenants do not agree on specifics or, at least, be inconvenient if one cannot be reached.

While joint tenancy financial assets, such as bank accounts, can be set up on an either/or basis, so that only one signature is required for transactions, this usually cannot be done with real estate. If one of the joint tenants becomes incompetent, either a guardianship or a durable power of attorney for property would be required to transfer the asset.

Let's examine what can happen after Dad dies and Mom puts the house in joint tenancy with her son, in the hope that it will pass to him after her death without probate. Such an arrangement can lead to potential disasters:

- If the son files for bankruptcy, is involved in a divorce proceeding, or is otherwise sued, the house could be lost, even though the son had nothing to do with its purchase and does not live in the house.
- Mother and son might become estranged. With joint tenancy, he would have as much right to decide how the house is used as she does.

- The son could predecease his mother, throwing her estate into probate when she dies.
- When the son becomes outright owner of the house after his mother's death, he need not respect her intentions. Perhaps she has three children and meant for the proceeds from the sale of the house to be shared equally. If the son who was named joint tenant decides he'd rather take the whole thing for himself, his siblings might have no legal recourse.
- If the son is married and he and his spouse are living in the house, the spouse's signature might be required for sale because they have marital rights. But what if their marriage is on the rocks and the spouse refuses to cooperate?
- Tax consequences must be carefully analyzed.

When crossing your "t's" and dotting your "i's," don't settle for simple "joint tenancy" if you intend the joint tenant to receive the entire asset upon your death: make sure the words "with rights of survivorship" appear as part of the title, particularly if a non-spouse is the joint tenant.

Tax Consequences of Non-Spousal Joint Tenancy

Another potential problem with the use of intergenerational joint tenancies—either parent and child, or grandparent and grandchild—are various tax consequences.

Income Tax Consequences

To understand the income tax implications of joint tenancies, it's necessary to comprehend the way the government taxes capital gains. When an asset increases in value between the time it is purchased and the time it is sold, capital gains taxes generally must be paid on the profit.

This is true whether the asset in question is a share of stock, a house, a piece of art, or just about anything else, although real estate does receive favorable tax treatment under certain circumstances. Just take the sale price, subtract the cost basis—that is, the initial cost of the asset plus money invested in it since, such as home-improvement costs, in the case of real estate—and you have the amount subject to the capital gains tax.

For highly appreciated assets, such as real estate or stocks owned for long periods of time, this tax can represent a substantial portion of the total value of the asset.

The government provides a measure of relief from these taxes when an appreciated asset is transferred by reason of its owner's death. In that case, the cost basis of the asset is "stepped up" to its value at the owner's date of death. Upon subsequent sale by the new owner, income tax is paid only on the appreciation following the date of death of the owner that the asset is inherited from. Any appreciation during the previous owner's lifetime escapes income tax.

Let's take a simplified example: Assume your parents bought shares of a certain stock for $10,000 decades ago. You inherited the stock upon the death of a parent two years ago, when it was worth $250,000. This year you decided to sell it, when the total value was at $275,000. You don't have to pay capital gains taxes on the $240,000 profit over your parents' purchase price, just on the final $25,000 increase in value.

This all adds up to a pretty hefty tax advantage for appreciated assets transferred at death. If an asset were gifted during the donor's lifetime, there would be no step-up in cost basis. Upon a subsequent sale of the asset by the person who received the gift, whether before or after the death of the original donor, capital gains taxes then would be required on the entire appreciation from the time of the original purchase.

How does this affect joint tenants? In part, it depends on the type of asset. For bank and brokerage accounts, the formation of a joint tenancy is not an immediate gift, unless a noncontributing joint tenant withdraws assets. Assets so withdrawn receive no step-up upon the death of the contributor. As to other assets, such as a house, the formation of the joint tenancy may be an immediate gift and lose a half step-up, depending on IRS treatment. Usually, if the surviving joint tenant made no contribution to the asset, then the asset is 100 percent includible in the contributing joint tenant's estate, and there would be a full step-up. However, there may be circumstances where the IRS would deny such a step-up, leading to potential capital gains taxes.

Often a child's name is put on an asset as a joint tenant for convenience purposes only, and the facts will dictate whether a gift has actually been made. Paradoxically, the filing of a federal gift-tax return may result in negative implications regarding future step-ups. However, if the gift tax return is required and no filing is made, penalties can be assessed. The IRS can go either way on these types of "transfers," depending on various factors, including the type of asset, whether proper filings are made, local law, and even which agent is doing the audit.

Step-Up Loophole Closed

Perhaps you've noticed that the step-up rules appear to open an even greater tax-saving loophole: If you have a family member likely to die before you, it could make sense to transfer highly appreciated assets to this person. Then have that family member leave the asset to you, thereby getting the advantages of the step-up without going through the trouble of dying.

The government has substantially closed this loophole by adding an exception to the step-up rules—namely, the one-year rule: if appreciated property is transferred to a donee who dies within one year of the transfer, and the donor or the donor's spouse indirectly benefits, the step-up may be negated.

Estate Tax Relating to Joint Tenancy

If you are fortunate enough to have estate tax problems, see chapters 10, 11, and 12. Suffice to say here that assets passing via joint tenancy do not escape estate taxes, except to the extent that the asset held in joint tenancy was, in fact, funded by the surviving joint tenant.

The general rule is that the entire value of a joint-tenancy asset is included in the taxable estate of the first joint tenant to die, except to the extent that the surviving joint tenant can prove a contribution toward the purchase of the asset. If non-spousal joint tenants sell and reinvest joint tenancy assets, proving contribution by one joint tenant or another becomes exceedingly complex and can be subject to scrutiny by the IRS, which is not known to be sympathetic to the difficulties inherent in the process.

A potential nightmare of non-spousal joint tenancies is double taxation. A joint tenancy asset can be taxed in the estate of the first joint tenant to die, to the extent that the surviving joint tenant cannot prove contribution—and then it can be taxed again in the surviving tenant's estate.

So when is non-spousal joint tenancy between a parent and a child appropriate? Generally, only when all of the following are true:
• There is only one surviving or competent parent and only one child (or other close relation);
• The child is unmarried;
• The child is an adult and can be trusted implicitly;
• The parent has more than enough assets, even without the assets in the joint tenancy; or
• The parent is relatively elderly—that is, likely to be within a few years of death.

Tenancy by the Entirety

Some states provide for a form of ownership, usually real estate, called tenancy by the entirety (T/E). A T/E is similar to a joint tenancy with rights of survivorship, in that upon the death of one of the tenants the asset held in T/E automatically passes to the survivor without probate. The main difference from joint tenancy is that a tenancy by the entirety may be created only by a married couple and may be severed only by agreement of both spouses. In Illinois, T/E can be used only for real estate and only for the couple's principal residence. Its primary advantage over a joint tenancy is that it shields the T/E asset from creditors who have a claim against just one spouse.

Tenancy by the entirety can be a useful asset-protection tool when one or both spouses are employed in professions susceptible to lawsuits. A T/E asset is not protected if a liability is joint between the spouses. Furthermore, upon the death of the first spouse to die, if the surviving spouse has liabilities, the creditors could then get to the asset.

Some states allow for the T/E assets to be owned by a joint or community property Trust and between two separate Trusts where the grantors and the beneficiaries are the spouses.

As we saw in this chapter, there are numerous ways to avoid probate, including the use of Trusts. Some of the shortcut methods, such as joint tenancies and tenancy by the entirety, may be simple and inexpensive to set up—yet do only half the job. Will money saved now result in an estate drain upon your death? ●

Action Plan Seven: Don't Stop Now!

Keep your family out of court:
1. Today, review the way your assets are owned. Consider whether they will avoid probate upon your death (and if you are married, if they will avoid probate upon the death of the surviving spouse).
2. If your assets are held in joint tenancy as a convenience only, consider that this convenience

Action Plan Seven: Don't Stop Now!

can be outweighed by horrendous results. A typical situation that has your deceased spouse "spinning in her grave" occurs when you put your house into joint tenancy with your second spouse, who survives you, because they will not be legally obligated to share that asset with your children from your first marriage. Strictly moral obligations, like sharing with a deceased spouse's children, mean next to nothing in a court of law.
3. Compare the potential financial costs of probate with the amount that a complete estate plan, including a Trust, will cost you.
4. Consider the loss of privacy in a probate proceeding. Would it bother you that anyone interested in looking at your probate file can see an inventory of your assets, along with the names and the addresses of your beneficiaries?

CHAPTER 8

Revocable Living Trusts

*"Put not your trust in money,
but put your money in Trust."*
—Oliver Wendell Holmes, Jr.

A Trust is a right of property, real or personal, held by one party for the benefit of another, or, in the case of a revocable trust, it may be created by, may be controlled by, and may benefit the same person acting in different roles (grantor, trustee, beneficiary).

Trusts can be created for any purpose, so long as that purpose is not illegal or against public policy, and if it is revocable, it can be changed by the grantor, the person who created it, at any time while living and competent.

You can avoid probate with a fully funded revocable Trust. To establish a Trust, you need:

- A beneficiary;
- A trustee who has fiduciary responsibilities toward the beneficiary with respect to the property—someone willing to look after the beneficiary's interests when it comes to the assets and be held to a high standard in doing so; and
- Property identified as belonging to the Trust and actually delivered to the Trust.

Revocable living Trusts are also sometimes known as living or inter vivos Trusts (Latin for "between living persons"), though some living trusts are, in fact, *irrevocable* upon creation. By any name, a *revocable* Trust is distinct from other forms of Trusts, in that the Trust may be amended or revoked by the grantor during the grantor's lifetime.

When people think of Trusts, they often think of banks. Many banks have Trust departments that can act as trustee for all types of Trusts. However, you can create a "self-declaration of Trust," where you, the grantor, act as your own trustee or co-trustee. You name the successor trustee to act on your behalf should you become incapacitated or die. Unless you choose to avail yourself of the expertise offered by a professional trustee, no bank need be involved with your Trust in any way.

Four words describe a revocable self-declaration of Trust:
You Control It Completely!

A revocable self-declaration of Trust can be a very useful estate-planning tool—the centerpiece of many estate plans. You no longer own certain assets directly; rather, you own and control them as trustee of your Trust. Trusts don't die; they continue until they exhaust or completely distribute their assets.

This might seem like mere semantics—and in some ways it is—but it has a number of benefits. For example, should you become incapacitated, your Trust is still as healthy as ever. And, properly constructed, it can operate in your absence. The successor trustee you have named in the Trust simply takes over the job of managing the assets in the Trust, according to whatever rules or guidelines you've laid out. As a result, the courts do not need to be involved through a probate proceeding, and there's no point at which the assets are out of your control or the control of your designated successor trustee.

Mechanics of a Revocable Living Trust

In order for a revocable Trust to be an efficient way to avoid both probate and loss of control over your assets, it must be "funded." Funding a self-declaration of Trust with your assets means transferring the assets from your name as an individual or a joint tenant to your name as trustee of your revocable Trust or effectively naming the Trust as a payable (or transferable) on death beneficiary.

After the creation of the Trust, take title to newly acquired assets as trustee as well, or name the Trust as beneficiary. Except to the extent that other, perhaps more sophisticated, estate-tax or creditor-protection strategies dictate otherwise, all real estate, no matter where it is located, should be transferred into the Trust, avoiding multiple "ancillary" probates in every state where you own real estate.

HOW TO DEFEAT PROCRASTINATION

Make deadlines, and mark them in your calendar. If you walk out of your attorney's office with your new Trust and do not do the follow-up work of funding it, much of your planning has been wasted, so set yourself a deadline, mark your calendar accordingly, and, if necessary, get help.

Because you control your Trust completely, you continue to control the assets owned by the Trust. If you want to change, sell, or spend Trust assets, you simply do it. The only difference is that instead of transacting business as an individual or a joint tenant, you now do so as a trustee.

So what will change? Not much. You may be required to add the word *trustee* to your signature, but most financial institutions don't require that. There is no additional bookkeeping required.

Income, gains, and losses flow through to you as an individual or a married couple, and the figures plug right into your regular 1040 tax form the same as they did before you established your Trust. If you file a joint return, you can continue to do so. No special tax ID number is required during your lifetime—you can continue to use your social security number on all of your accounts.

There are no ongoing fees associated with maintaining a revocable self-declaration of Trust. Unless you later need to amend the Trust, the cost of the revocable living Trust is a relatively modest one-time expense. Upon your death, your next-named successor trustee gains control over your assets according to your written directions, without any involvement by the probate court.

Benefits of a Fully Funded Revocable Living Trust

A fully funded revocable living Trust often serves as the centerpiece of a complete estate plan. It accomplishes the essential purposes of a Will—to distribute your assets to your beneficiaries upon death—smoothly, without probate.

You do not give up any control of the assets in the Trust while living. A revocable living Trust will provide for a successor trustee to begin acting upon your death or during any period of incompetence. When you do die, your assets will be distributed per your instructions or will continue to be controlled within the Trust—whatever you direct in the Trust document.

The reason the process works so smoothly is simple: The Trust owns the assets, and a Trust does not die or become incompetent. It continues under a new set of circumstances already anticipated in the Trust instrument, with different people in control for the benefit of new beneficiaries. The Trust can continue during your surviving spouse's lifetime, during the lifetimes of your children and grandchildren—even if they are not yet born at the time of your death.

If your revocable living Trust is fully funded with your assets, there will likely be no probate when you die. Your successor trustee or heirs might choose to consult with a lawyer to understand your Trust, but even so, the legal fees involved in the process are often reduced dramatically because no assets have to pass through probate and, thus, no lawyers will have to go to court.

Funding Your Trust

Some initial paperwork will be required to transfer assets to the Trust or change beneficiary designations of your assets. This is known as funding the Trust and can be compared to pre-probating your own estate without using a court. You can have your attorney handle the funding from start to finish, or you can lower your legal fees by having them simply provide you with guidelines to assist you with making the changes on your own, in conjunction with your financial advisers.

By avoiding probate, a revocable living Trust is more difficult to contest than a probated Will. Any person who has standing to make a claim in court, such as a potential beneficiary or creditor, can contest a Will or make a claim against the probate assets. The probate court will disregard a Will if it finds:

1. It is technically defective, such as lacking required signatures, witnesses, or notarization;
2. There is a finding of undue influence by someone, usually a beneficiary, over the testator (the person whose Will is being probated); or
3. The testator lacked capacity when signing the Will.

The attacker of a fully funded revocable living Trust, where no probate is required to transfer Trust assets to beneficiaries, must initiate the battle by filing a court action in a legal forum other than probate court.

Examples: With and without a Revocable Living Trust

Compare your estate with a fully funded revocable living Trust versus either not creating or not funding a revocable living Trust.

The differences depend on your personal situation. If you have a relatively small estate, the effect of failing to implement and fund a revocable living Trust might be little more than a few time-consuming tasks for your family. But if you have a large estate, your procrastination might lead to hefty probate-related fees or cost you opportunities for estate-tax savings, a topic we'll cover in more depth in chapter 10.

Here's a look at a few examples of how your probate assets flow upon death:

Example 1

No Will, no funded Trust:

- You may have created significant problems for those you've left behind.
- The probate process begins.
- The court appoints an administrator who may or may not be the person you would have selected.
- After your heirs post a surety bond, likely costing them hundreds or even thousands of dollars yearly, the court supervises the payment of all your debts.
- Various court costs and legal fees will be paid, draining 2 to 10 percent of the value of your estate, perhaps much more.
- After a minimum period of time (six months in Illinois), distribution of your remaining assets is made according to a preset formula of intestate succession, making no distinction between specific needs of your heirs and not taking your intentions into account.

- Until probate is finished, it may be difficult for your heirs to make transactions related to your accounts.
- Meanwhile, anyone who wishes to take a look at the estate may do so simply by requesting the probate file at the court.
- If you have a spouse and children, they share your assets, even if your children are very young.

Example 2

No revocable Trust, but you leave a Will:
- The executor will be the one you select, and the assets will go to the persons or the charities you picked, in the percentages or the amounts stated in your Will.
- Assuming no one disputes your Will, you waive the surety bond requirement, and you permit independent administration in the Will, probate fees will be kept to a minimum.
- If there are no special circumstances, such as beneficiaries disputing your wishes, the probate will be fairly smooth.
- The drawback will be that your Will is open to public examination, and at least six months will elapse before your heirs fully inherit.

Example 3

Your assets are owned by a revocable living Trust:
- At your death, the successor trustee can immediately and without court order direct the bank and the broker to act in whatever terms you've laid out in the Trust.
- There are no court costs or court-related attorney fees.
- The assets are never in a probate twilight zone.
- There is no public probate record of your assets.

Selecting a Trustee: Banks versus Individuals

If you're acting as your own trustee with a self-declaration of Trust, you can name either an individual or a corporate trustee, such as a bank's Trust department, as successor trustee. Of course, you don't want to name anyone or any institution as a possible trustee if you don't trust the individual's or the institution's ethics or judgment.

After you select one or more individuals as successor trustee (after yourself), you may also select one or more additional backups, in case your original choice or choices cannot act (e.g., if they die before you or with you or become incapacitated).

You can select individual co-trustees who would work together, but be careful about using more than two or three; above that, your co-trustee structure might create gridlock. While you are living and competent, you can change your choice of trustee at any time, just as you can change any of the Trust's other terms.

Some attorneys offer themselves as successor trustee to their clients. Whether this is appropriate or not may depend on the type of relationship you have with the lawyer. A longtime family lawyer who is intimate with your family's dynamics may make a great trustee or co-trustee, but if your relationship is just beginning or the lawyer is a sole practitioner without a succession plan of their own, that person may not be the best choice.

If you decide that a professional trustee is the best choice, consider the resources available to the trustee. In my opinion, banks are usually better suited than law firms when it comes to investing Trust assets and distributing money to heirs.

It's also reasonable to give your beneficiaries the authority to select or remove the bank. If the bank is "untouchable," it may act coldly toward your beneficiaries, whereas if it can be removed, it may be more responsive.

When selecting an individual trustee (and the same reasoning applies when selecting an agent for property or an executor), look for two qualities:

- First, you obviously want someone who is trustworthy—who won't steal the money from the beneficiaries.

- Second, you want someone who is going to live up to the responsibility—not put the bank and brokerage statements in a drawer and forget about them.

If you're concerned that an individual you wish to select as trustee might be overwhelmed by the complexity of the Trust—an argument that bank Trust departments often use to encourage the use of their services—simply grant them the authority to hire a bank, an attorney, or a CPA for help in managing the Trust or to appoint a co-trustee.

Another valid argument banks make is that emotional family issues sometimes require the detachment of an independent trustee. For example, if you're concerned your children might not get along with each other when it comes to handling your estate, a bank might be the most appropriate trustee. Perhaps naming one child as trustee might offend another, especially if that would leave one child in charge of distributing money to siblings. Such an arrangement can also lead to a conflict of interest to the child/ trustee who may be a remainder beneficiary of undistributed Trust assets to their siblings.

Consider making adult children trustee over their own Trust shares once the Trust divides. This minimizes the potential conflict between siblings but does not address the problem of one or more children with a history of making poor financial judgments.

Banks can be coldhearted institutions, but they don't get sick, die, or move away; they don't share old family grudges or rivalries; and they will understand the documents. For all of these reasons, banks are often the best choice as trustee.

Their drawback is cost. A typical yearly bank fee is likely to be in the neighborhood of 1 to 2 percent. That might not sound like much, but over time it can add up. Of course, the net cost of not using a professional trustee could be much higher than a bank fee if the individuals you select do a poor job. As intelligent as your individual trustee may be, the value of your estate could be more money than that person has handled before, and the job can be a daunting one.

Conversely, the fees charged by banks often make them inappropriate for small Trust estates.

- As a rule of thumb, unless your estate is worth more than $250,000, the cost of a bank trustee may be prohibitive. Some banks have minimum Trust account sizes that might be more than the estate value.
- If the value of your Trust is under $1 million and you prefer to use a bank as trustee, it might make sense to consider a local, suburban bank, rather than a behemoth, where costs and minimum account sizes generally are higher, and the amount of attention paid to small Trusts may be less.

Liability issues also should be considered. If an individual trustee dissipates Trust assets, that person may be legally liable to your beneficiaries, but it does them no good if the trustee hasn't got the money to pay them. However, if a bank ruins a Trust, your heirs would have a better chance to recover the assets in a lawsuit. Banks generally have deep pockets and are insured for things like negligence or even theft by an employee.

Investment Policy Statement

For clear communications and as protection from liability, it is useful for a trustee to state, in writing, an investment policy. It also helps to protect the trustee who is following a roadmap.

Such a document can articulate objectives such as investment guidelines, risk tolerance, performance goals, diversification requirements, communication expectations, and review parameters. Having a written statement is especially useful when the Trust's performance is inadequate compared to the overall market because it may be used to explain the trustee's actions to a disgruntled beneficiary. A financial professional working with the trustee's lawyer can help the trustee draft an investment-policy statement. ●

Action Plan Eight: You're Making Progress!

A three-step plan for creating and maintaining your Trust:

- Decide whom you would like to have as a trustee. Is one of your children particularly responsible or good with money? If none of them would make an appropriate choice, what about a sibling or a lifelong friend? Consider whether selecting one of your children over another would drive a wedge into their relationship.

- Would a professional trustee such as a bank be more suitable, for example, if your estate is large or complex or if family dynamics are a consideration? If so, call this week for a meeting with your bank's Trust representative, and discuss how the bank would handle your Trust.

- If you have a Trust, make sure it is funded correctly. If you have not followed the steps required to fund your Trust, begin the process this week. Gather your bank, brokerage, mutual fund, and other statements and start doing the appropriate paperwork. If you need help, call your attorney or financial adviser. Request change of ownership and change of beneficiary forms within one week, and also set a deadline in your calendar for one month from today to complete the process. With regard to beneficiary designations, request and keep a record from the financial company of the beneficiaries, including all contingents, with either your estate-plan documents or your financial records or both.

CHAPTER 9

Deciding Who Gets What and How

"When you have to make a choice and don't make it, that in itself is a choice."
—William James

Proceeding with a revocable living Trust means making some decisions about who gets your assets when you die. The Trust can divide your estate and direct payment to your beneficiaries according to almost any legitimate formula creative minds can devise.

Many people without a surviving spouse provide that upon death, their assets are divided into equal shares and immediately distributed to their grown children. If the children are not competent adults, restrictions can be added on how the assets benefit them, and additional provisions can pass benefits on to grandchildren and further descendants.

Others—if they have no children, have children with differing levels of need, have poor relationships with certain children, or have very close friends or other relatives they wish to consider— devise their own formulas. Some states require that a certain percentage of your assets be given to a surviving spouse, but in most states there is absolutely no law demanding you include or exclude any individual.

You simply need to explain the details in your Will or Trust. If you leave someone out, you might consider briefly explaining your thinking as well, so there's no confusion or hurt feelings, but this is certainly not required. Language such as "for reasons best known to my son, Bob, he gets nothing" can suffice or, even better, for total estrangement from a family line may be "Neither my son, Bob, nor any of my son Bob's descendants shall be deemed to have survived me."

THINK

When favoring one child over another in some manner, either by giving one child more assets than the other or by giving one child more authority than the other, take some time to consider the effect this may have on future family relations. Sibling rivalry has been around as long as Cain and Abel. Do you want to fan the flames of sibling rivalry, keeping it alive into the next generation?

Limiting the Use of Your Money

One way to protect your assets while giving control to your children is to make each of your adult children trustee of his or her own share of the estate, keeping the assets in Trust, instead of turning them over outright. You can impose further restrictions by making the principal off limits, giving your children access only to the income generated by the Trust and perhaps additional distributions for select purposes, such as health care, education, emergencies, or purchase of a house.

Such provisions are not overly restrictive but provide some protection from outside influences. Because the child/trustee does not own the assets outright, the assets may be shielded from your child's creditors or from the child's spouse, if handled correctly, and may also be excluded from the child's estate at death. Language such as this may allow for generation skipping (chapter 12), in effect making the gift to your grandchildren while still giving your children access to the money during their lifetimes in such a way that the gift is not includable in their own estates. However, to strengthen those aspects of the Trust that protect it from outside influences, it may be better to name a trustee other than the child to handle their share.

Some other options:

- You can tie your children's access to the money in the Trust to their age, so that they gain some access at 18, perhaps, but don't receive full access until age 25 (or 70 or never). Similar provisions can apply to any contingent beneficiaries, such as grandchildren or great nieces and nephews.

- Instead of age, you can tie full access to time, such as giving the child control over a portion of the principal upon your death, followed by another portion 5 and 10 years down the line. You can stretch it out over a long period and couple it with an age over which the child gains control regardless of the incremental time period.

- You can define what type of payments you want the trustee to make on your beneficiary's behalf, such as for education, health-care, or housing expenses.

- You can create incentives so that the beneficiary receives assets when a certain goal is achieved, such as attaining a college degree.

- If you have a beneficiary with special needs, you will want to ensure that their lifetime needs will be taken care of by a trustee, above and beyond what the government provides, but without resulting in a monetary disqualification of benefits. We'll cover special needs Trusts in chapter 12.

- You can grant broad rights to the money, but even if you trust your heirs to use it properly, expanding the rights of withdrawal or, worse, mandating a payout can give creditors and spouses easier access and cost the Trust its ability to skip to your grandchildren's generation for estate-tax purposes.

Dealing with Personal Property

Most families can divide personal possessions without too many ugly feelings or bloodshed. Unfortunately, that's not always the case because they are not like money, which can be evenly divided. Sometimes multiple beneficiaries want to inherit the same treasured memento. Families have blown up over a single photo album.

The solution varies from family to family. Many people prefer to let the beneficiaries decide among themselves who gets what. If they cannot agree, you can direct:

1. The executor or the trustee to sell the items the beneficiaries cannot agree on and split the money.
2. The executor or the trustee to donate the contested items to charity.
3. The executor or the trustee to decide who gets what.

You can specifically bequeath each item to a particular individual through your Will or revocable living Trust, but this requires considerable detail. Besides, are you going to change your Will or Trust every time you acquire something new or give something away while you are still alive? One compromise is to maintain a separate list, which you mention in your Trust, that details how you want your personal items distributed. You can change the list anytime you want. In most states the separate list that you maintain is not legally enforceable if it is directing probate assets pursuant to a Will unless it is signed with the same witnessing requirements prescribed for Wills in your state.

Generally, Trusts do not require the same formality in dealing with tangible personal property as Wills.

A Will or a Trust is also a good place to mention any particular items that you'd prefer to see go to a close friend, rather than your family.

Other techniques:

1. Videotape your possessions and narrate who gets what.
2. Set up a "round robin" to allow the beneficiaries to choose items for themselves, each selecting one item per round, as you would choose up sides for a neighborhood baseball game. Reverse the order for round 2. Specify whom you'd like included in this process and perhaps who goes first, or they can cut cards. Is it just your children? What if one of your children predeceases you? Should that child's children then participate in the division? What about your siblings or any close friends and relatives?
3. Any other game of chance that works for the beneficiaries.

Consulting Descendants about Personal Property

Some experts advise those doing estate planning to ask their children which items of personal property they might want. The theory is that it's better to sort such issues out ahead of time, rather than create potential squabbles later.

This may well work for your family, but there's a trap here. Some children don't like to think about their parents' death. Others don't want to show any interest for fear that they will seem greedy. Some kids may start battling right from the get-go. As a result of any of these pitfalls, the entire estate-planning process might stall. If you attempt to sort out your personal property with the assistance of your children and they delay the process, move on. Don't let their procrastination be your downfall.

REAL-LIFE STORIES

Twelve years ago, Joyce died, leaving a husband, Henry, 52; a daughter, Emily, 17; and a son, Tom, 14. She also left an impressive collection of heirloom jewelry handed down from mother to daughter. When Joyce died, Henry took control of the jewelry, with every intention of passing it along to Emily when she wed, as Joyce had directed. But before Emily married, Henry remarried, then died without a Will. Joyce's jewelry was divided between Henry's second wife, a wicked stepmother, according to Emily and Tom, who received half. Emily and Tom received 25 percent each. The stepmother gave her share of the jewelry to her own daughters. Tom couldn't care less about the jewelry and sold his portion. When Emily married and had a daughter a few years later, she did the necessary estate planning to protect what was left of her mother's ancestors' precious heirlooms

---

If you have substantial personal property that might be sold after your death, it could be worth your while to suggest a method of selling it. This is particularly appropriate if your children or the person in charge of liquidating the property understands neither its value nor ways to maximize that value.

Reputable estate-sale companies and auction houses are knowledgeable about dealing with such substantial assets as jewelry, art, antiques, or period furniture. If something might otherwise be sold for garage-sale prices, leave instructions for your heirs to consult with expert resources.

The Pour-Over Will

A fully funded revocable living Trust can be a great estate-planning tool, the Swiss Army knife of your estate plan, but it does not stand alone. A complete estate plan also requires a durable power of attorney for property and for health-care directives (both discussed in chapter 7) and a pour-over Will.

A pour-over Will is a special type of Will used in conjunction with a revocable living Trust. It "pours" any asset not titled in the name of your revocable living Trust into your Trust upon your death. As with all Wills, it activates only upon your death.

The pour-over Will does not need to be a complex document, but it should, like any other Will:

1. Revoke any prior Wills.
2. Distribute any personal and household effects that have not already been distributed in your Trust or elsewhere.
3. Appoint an executor to take control of your assets and distribute them per your wishes.
4. Name a guardian for any minor children.
5. Give directions regarding the funeral, and so on.
6. Instead of directing your estate to particular beneficiaries, the pour-over Will directs the executor to transfer any remaining assets into your Trust.

Having a pour-over Will as part of your comprehensive estate plan minimizes the impact of probate, while ensuring that your assets will be distributed in the manner that you state in your revocable Trust. This is true even if you have not transferred all your assets into your Trust prior to your death. However, when you have a revocable Trust, you want your Will to process as few assets as possible. The more that the revocable Trust is funded, the less work the pour-over Will does.

Guardianship of Minor Children

You know that if you die without an estate plan, you'll have no say in who looks after your children in your absence. Your Will, whether a pour-over Will used in conjunction with a Trust or a traditional Will, should name a guardian for any children who are under the age of majority—generally 18, but varying from state to state.

Your selection of a guardian is a preference based in large measure on lifestyle considerations. Who would give the most love and impart the best value system to your children? Who would your children feel most comfortable living with? What living arrangement would be least disruptive to your children's everyday routine? The answers to these questions are very subjective, very personal—and very important to your estate planning and peace of mind.

The selection of a guardian for your minor children is not an absolute right. It is actually a nomination made by you to the probate court through your Will, with the court reserving final judgment over the matter. However, courts give considerable weight to responsible selections made by parents. As with all fiduciary appointments and nominations, it is good practice to name backups, in case the first or even second person(s) selected cannot act.

If your children have a surviving parent, that person will typically be appointed by the court even if you nominate someone else, unless there is a very substantial reason to defeat that person's parental rights—for example, if they are a criminal or a drug addict.

If you would seek to defeat someone's parental rights, provide as much information as possible to enable the court to make a ruling favorable to your way of thinking, but don't include anything that could be seen as a defamation of character, or your estate could wind up at the wrong end of a lawsuit. Keep it as specific as possible. Don't just make broad statements about the surviving parent's poor character. Give hard facts that can be documented, such as court file numbers, arrests, convictions, and incarcerations.

Guardianship details people sometimes overlook:

1. If naming more than one guardian nominated, determine what should happen if one of them dies or, if married, they split up. You can specify that you want them to act as guardians only if they are able to do so collectively, or that one or the other shall be permitted to act individually.

2. You may want your children to be consulted on the choice of guardian, depending on their ages at the time the decision must be made. Along those same lines, you can specify that an older child who has reached a predetermined majority age may act as guardian.

3. You may specify that certain guardians shall act only if they are willing to take all of your children.

4. If religion is an issue, you can consider whether a potential guardian is willing to raise your children according to your beliefs (or to continue to expose them to the faiths of both you and your spouse, if different).

5. You may want to state specifically that both sides of the family shall have reasonable access to the children and keep them away from the toxic relatives whom you avoid.

Any of these things, and more, can be included in the Will. Your ultimate choice of guardian can be based on any number of factors, but it doesn't need to be based on financial considerations. Your trustee can be instructed to make payments as needed so that your children are not a financial burden to their guardian.

Let's say you prefer your brother, who lives in a modest house, as guardian. Your Trust could be structured to pay for an addition to his house to accommodate your children. This could be a gift, or, with a well-drafted estate plan, the increased value may become part of your Trust, which is paid back later, when the house is sold. You can also provide that the guardian, the guardian's family, and your children can live in your house while your children are growing up.

HOW TO DEFEAT PROCRASTINATION

Do the simplest part first so you can get moving. Once you're moving—once you've made some decisions—it's easier to continue.

Should you name the same person(s) as both guardian and trustee? An argument can be made either way. It may be most convenient if the guardian is also the trustee. And, if you trust the guardian with raising your children, you should trust that person with the children's money, too, right?

Maybe yes, maybe no. The guardian is usually not required to provide too much detail regarding the day-to-day expenses related to your children because keeping track of such items as the cost of food and other incidentals may be unnecessarily difficult. An allowance could be agreed on between the guardian and the trustee, with additional requests being made for "big-ticket" items, such as private school tuition, orthodonture, or other large expenditures. For the big-ticket payments, the guardian submits the bills to the trustee, who pays them directly from the Trust funds. Such items should be accounted for whether or not the trustee and the guardian are the same person. If the same person has all the qualities to be both trustee and guardian, the main reason for their being different people is if you feel that a separation of duties is necessary to protect your children. ●

SHORT-TERM GUARDIANSHIP

Let's say you are going camping in a remote location for a week and leaving your children with Grandma. Your son falls on the playground and breaks an arm. Grandma might have a difficult time dealing with the emergency without specific permission from a parent. Illinois provides a useful form known as a Statutory Form for Appointment of Short-Term Guardian. Check with your attorney: Does your state have a form that will accomplish the same goal?

ILLINOIS STATUTORY SHORT FORM
APPOINTMENT OF SHORT-TERM GUARDIAN

[IT IS IMPORTANT TO READ THE FOLLOWING INSTRUCTIONS:

By properly completing this form, a parent or the guardian of the person of the child is appointing a guardian of a child of the parent (or a minor ward of the guardian, as the case may be) for a period of up to 365 days. A separate form should be completed for each child. The person appointed as the guardian must sign the form, but need not do so at the same time as the parent or parents or guardian.

This form may not be used to appoint a guardian if there is a guardian already appointed for the child, except that if a guardian of the person of the child has been appointed, that guardian may use this form to appoint a short-term guardian. Both living parents of a child may together appoint a guardian of the child, or the guardian of the person of the child may appoint a guardian of the child, for a period of up to 365 days through the use of this form. If the short-term guardian is appointed by both living parents of the child, the parents need not sign the form at the same time .]

1. Parent (or guardian) and Child. I, _____, currently residing at _____
_____, am a parent
(or guardian of the person) of the following child (or a child likely to be born):

   Name: _____
(or "not yet born")

   Birthdate: _____
(or expected birthdate)

2. Guardian.   I hereby appoint the following person as the short term guardian for the child:

   Name: _____
   Address: _____
   _____
   _____

3. Effective Date. This appointment becomes effective: (check one if you wish it to be applicable):

_____ On the date that I state in writing that I am no longer either willing or able to make and carry out day-to day child care decisions concerning the child.

_____ On the date that a physician familiar with my condition certifies in writing that I am no longer willing or able to make and carry out day-to-day child care decisions concerning the child.

_____ On the date that I am admitted as an in-patient to a hospital or other health care institution.

_____ On the following date: _____.

_____ Other: _____
_____
_____
_____
_____

[Note: If this item is not completed, the appointment is effective immediately upon the date the form is signed and dated below.]

4. Termination. This appointment shall terminate 365 days after the effective date, unless it terminates sooner as determined by the event or date I have indicated below: (check one if you wish it to be applicable.)

_____ On the date that I stated in writing that I am willing and able to make and carry out day-to-day child care decisions concerning the child.

_____ On the date that a physician familiar with my condition certifies in writing that I am willing and able to make and carry out day-to-day child care decisions concerning the child.

_____ On the date that I am discharged from the hospital or other health care institution where I was admitted as an in-patient, which established the effective date.

_____ On the date which is _____ days (state a number of days, but no more than 365 days) after the effective date.

_____ Other: _____

_____

_____

_____

[Note: If this item is not completed, the appointment will be effective for a period of 365 days, beginning on the effective date.]

5. Date and signature of appointing parent or guardian.

This appointment is made this _____ day of _____ 200_____
                               (day)   (month)   (year)

Signed: _____
                        (appointing parent or guardian)

6. Witnesses.

I saw the parent (or the guardian of the person of the child) sign this instrument or I saw the parent (or guardian of the person of the child) direct someone to sign this instrument for the parent (or the guardian). Then I signed this instrument as a witness in the presence of the parent (or the guardian). I am not appointed in this instrument to act as the short-term guardian for the child.

Witness: _____
                    (name)

_____

_____
                    (address)

Witness: _____
                    (name)

_____

_____
                    (address)

7. Acceptance of Short-Term Guardian. I accept this appointment as short-term guardian.

On this _____ day of _____ , 20 _____.
     (day)   (month)   (year)

Signed: _____
        (short-term guardian)

8. Consent of Child's Other Parent. I, _____
_____ , currently residing at
_____ ,
hereby consent to this appointment.

On this _____ day of   _____ 20 _____.
    (day)   (month)   (year)

Signed: _____
        (consenting parent)

[Note: The signature of a consenting parent is not necessary if one of the following applies:

(i) the child's other parent has died; or
(ii) the whereabouts of the child's other parent are not known; or
(iii) the child's other parent is not willing or able to make and carry out day-to-day child care decisions concerning the child; or
(iv) the child's parents were never married and no court has issued an order establishing parentage.]

Action Plan Nine: You Can Make Good Decisions!

A four-step strategy for making key decisions:

1. Think about how you want your personal property divided among your beneficiaries. If you want to specify particular items, make a list this week. If you want input from the beneficiaries regarding what items they want, ask them to make their own lists. Although some of the beneficiaries might find the whole process to be morbid, consider targeting the next family get-together as an occasion to let them stake their future claims.

2. Decide on a system to resolve potential disputes over items of personal property that are not specifically bequeathed. You can direct that the trustee have the discretion to sell such items or allow the trustee to make the determination regarding who gets what.

3. If you have young children and have made your preliminary guardianship decision, discuss the decision with the person you have selected, preferably before you sign your Will. Make an assessment as to whether the prospective guardian is willing to act under the parameters that you wish. If your children are old enough, discuss guardianship issues with them.

4. Take some time to think through whether each of your beneficiaries can be trusted to receive their inheritances outright or if some controls are needed.

5. When done correctly, your Trust and your Will (along with powers of attorney) fit together like pieces in a jigsaw puzzle.

CHAPTER 10

Looking Out for Estate Taxes

"In delay there lies no plenty."
—William Shakespeare

Those who fail to plan their estates let the probate court, which interprets state law, decide their personal and financial fate in the event of death and incapacity.

On top of that, without proper planning, if your assets place you near the top of the financial wealth pyramid or you live in a state where moderately affluent estates are taxed, the government might take a hefty slice for itself.

Federal estate taxes, also known as death taxes, affect less than .1 percent of the U.S. population who died in 2020, or one in a thousand. The threshold for federal estate taxes, known as the applicable exclusion amount, is $11.7 million per person. There are techniques, touched on below, available to a married couple, potentially allowing a doubling of that amount, to $23.4 million between them.

If no new laws governing estate taxes are passed prior to January 1, 2026, the threshold for taxes is cut in half, to $5.6 million per person, with inflation adjustors from January 1, 2017. If your estate is subject to a federal estate tax, the rate is 40 percent on the amount greater than the bassic exclusion amount.

Gifts to individuals greater than the annual exclusion amount in any year (currently $15,000) must be reported to the IRS, and the excess of the gift over the annual exclusion amount is subtracted from your basic exclusion amount.

If you are fortunate enough to have an estate-tax "problem," don't put off planning for it just because you don't have an April 15 deadline staring you in the face. You never know when you will breathe your last.

When calculating whether your estate will be subject to a federal estate tax, include all of your assets: life insurance death payout, retirement plans, the equity in your real estate, your valuable collections, the appraisal value of any businesses you own, in addition to all of your other holdings.

Techniques for Fortunate Couples to Double the Basic Exclusion Amount, Collectively, to $23.4 Million:

1. Married couples can balance their estates so that the "poorer" spouse has at least $11.7 million in assets, then establish a shelter Trust, discussed later in this chapter.
2. If the estate of the first-to-die spouse is under $11.75 million, but the surviving spouse faces a potential federal estate tax, then the survivor can file an estate tax return to utilize "portability," preserving the first-to-die spouse's DSUEA (Deceased Spouse's Unused Basic Exclusion Amount). This only works for married couples and is disregarded if the surviving spouse remarries.
3. Another postmortem estate tax–planning technique, disclaiming assets, is discussed later in this chapter.

Congratulations. If you have made it this far, take a break. You are doing a great job. Appreciate the gift of life, and do something you enjoy.

State Estate and Inheritance Taxes (2020)

Seventeen states plus Washington, D.C., confuse the estate tax picture further with taxes levied on either estates or inheritances, with one state, Maryland, taxing both.*

<u>Inheritance Tax States</u>

Iowa
Exemption amount: None
Top tax rate: 15%

Kentucky
Exemption amount: $500
Top tax rate: 16%

Maryland
No exemption, top rate is 10%.

Nebraska
Exemption amount: $10,000
Top tax rate: 18%

New Jersey
Exemption amount: $500
Top tax rate: 16%

Pennsylvania
Exemption amount: None
Top tax rate: 15%

The amount of inheritance tax generally depends on the relationship between the deceased and the inheritor. Some relations are not subject to the tax.

Estate Tax States (and Washington, D.C.)

Connecticut
Exemption amount: $5.1 million
Top tax rate: 12%
Cap: $15 million

Hawaii
Exemption amount: $5.49 million
Top rate: 20%

Illinois
Exemption amount: $4 million
Top tax rate: 16%

Maine
Exemption amount: $5.8 million
Top tax rate: 12%

Maryland
Exempt amount: $5 million
Top tax rate: 16%

Massachusetts
Exemption amount: $1 million
Top tax rate: 16%

Minnesota
Exemption amount: $3 million*
Top tax rate: 16%

New York
Exemption amount: $5,850 million
Top tax rate: 16%

Oregon
Exemption amount: $1 million
Top tax rate: 16%

Rhode Island
Exemption amount: $1,579,922
Top tax rate: 16%

Vermont
Exemption: $4.25 million
Top tax rate: 16%

Washington
Exemption amount: $2,193,000*
Top tax rate: 20%

Washington, D.C.
Exemption Amount: $5,762,400 million
Top rate: 16%

*Source: The American College of Trust and Estate Counsel

At one time, state estate and inheritance taxes were a minor irritation compared to the federal estate/death tax. Now, with federal estate taxes affecting far fewer people, many moderately wealthy retirees are migrating to states where the climate—both tax and weather—is most advantageous.

HOW TO DEFEAT PROCRASTINATION

Consider the cost of putting the task off.
What future problems or unnecessary expenses might be created now because you are not taking care of current business?

The Unlimited Marital Deduction

One way to postpone estate taxes, both federal and state, is the Unlimited Marital Deduction because gifts or bequests between spouses can exceed the maximum basic exclusion amount without any estate tax consequence.

You can also transfer any amount of money, tax-free, either during your lifetime or at your death, to your surviving spouse—providing that the receiving spouse is a U.S. citizen and that you are legally married, not just living together as if married.

Although the Unlimited Marital Deduction is referred to as a deduction, it more accurately might be called a blanket exclusion from all transfer taxes between husband and wife.

The primary problem with the Unlimited Marital Deduction lies in its overuse, particularly in states that have their own estate tax. When people learn they can leave their estates to their spouses without concern for estate taxes, they often assume this is the best option for most or all of their assets.

In fact, most married people have very simple estate plans. Their estates are structured so that upon one's death, all assets go outright to the surviving spouse. This may be an "I love you" plan, but it also might be a myopic plan. In effect, the couple may over-utilize their Unlimited Marital Deductions to the detriment of contingent beneficiaries.

It's a classic procrastination trap: In estates subject to a state or federal estate tax, overuse of the Unlimited Marital Deduction doesn't always avoid estate taxes. Without the use of portability and/or the use of disclaimers, it may only put the tax off until the second spouse dies—when the problem may be more difficult to solve. If the maximum basic exclusion amount of the first spouse-to-die is underfunded or lost, taxes can be due that could otherwise easily be avoided.

Portability

An alternative available for wealthy married couples that can allow them to avoid dividing their estates during their lifetime may be the use of portability, which preserves the deceased spouse's unused exclusion amount (DSUEA). In other words, the unused bassic exclusion amount of the "poorer" spouse who dies first can be subtracted from the taxable estate of the surviving spouse.

Though portability may make the division of some married couples' assets for estate-tax planning unnecessary, there are other considerations:

- Preserving the DSUEA requires the filing of an estate tax return upon the first spouse's death, even if the first-to-die spouse's estate is relatively small. On that return, the value of the first spouse's estate is left open until the second spouse dies. Then, if the survivor's estate exceeds the basic exclusion amount, before the survivor's estate is taxed any excess is used to fill the first-to-die spouse's remaining basic exclusion amount as it existed at the time of that first death.

- If it turns out that the survivor's estate is below the basic exclusion amount, then the legal/accounting fees spent preparing a tax return on the first death may have been a waste of time and money.

- It applies only to the most recent spouse's unused credit, so a survivor who remarries loses the DSUEA upon their subsequent death.

- Portability does not allow for growth. A shelter Trust funded with $11.7 million could grow to $20 million by the time it is paid to contingent beneficiaries, but portability would allow only for the subtraction of the DSUEA from the estate of the surviving spouse.

- It does not adjust for inflation.

- It works only for legally married couples.

- The generation-skipping tax exemption (chapter 12) is not portable.
- Many state estate taxes are not portable, so the strategy to avoid all estate taxes would still involve transferring enough assets to the poorer spouse if the richer spouse's estate exceeds the state estate-tax threshold and the poorer spouse dies first.

QDOT FOR FOREIGN SPOUSES

If the surviving spouse is not a U.S. citizen, they cannot benefit from the unlimited marital deduction. The U.S. government wants to prevent the surviving spouse from returning to their home country with an untaxed inheritance. Instead of a person being allowed to make unlimited gifts to a noncitizen spouse, the yearly maximum limit is $152,000.

Any assets passing to a non-citizen surviving spouse exceeding the basic exclusion amount must be put into a Qualified Domestic Trust, or QDOT, that names a domestic trustee for the assets. If the surviving spouse becomes a citizen within nine months after the death of the first spouse, a QDOT is unnecessary, but it ordinarily takes longer than nine months to process citizenship. Upon the death of the surviving spouse, assets in a QDOT will be subject to estate taxes.

Basic Exclusion Amount Shelter Trusts

Shelter Trusts work like this: First, the spouses sever most joint tenancies. That means major assets previously owned jointly by both spouses are now owned by either one or the other, in Trust or individually. Contact the financial institutions where your major accounts are held for instructions on severing joint tenancies, and ask your lawyer for instructions on dealing with other major assets, such as real estate.

Each spouse should individually control a basket of assets roughly equal to the basic exclusion amount (your state's, if any, first; then the federal amount). The remainder of the estate can be held in either spouse's Trust or in any way that seems most appropriate, perhaps in joint tenancy (although that can subject the estate to eventual probate upon the death of the survivor) or by some other entity.

Don't let your desire to hold a checking account or your automobile in joint tenancy with your spouse or another family member prevent you from setting up a Trust. It's okay to continue to hold a few relatively minor assets, such as a modest joint checking account, in joint tenancy.

When the first spouse dies, that person's basket of assets, up to the basic exclusion amount, will pass into a shelter Trust, discussed below.

The term *basic exclusion amount shelter Trust* best describes its function, although the term *family Trust* is what you will often see in a Trust document that utilizes the shelter Trust technique. The surviving spouse can benefit from the assets in the shelter Trust during the survivor's lifetime and can have significant, though not total, control over its assets.

If kept properly segregated, these assets never become part of the survivor's estate, and upon the survivor's death, the assets in the shelter Trust are distributed in accordance with the wishes of the first spouse to die. In this way, the estate-tax exemption of the first deceased spouse can be preserved, provided the surviving spouse follows the Trust's directions and does not commingle the shelter Trust assets with other assets.

A few other details need to be considered: It might be necessary to change beneficiary designations of contractual assets, such as insurance. Care must be given to the beneficiary designations of

IRAs and qualified plans. Retirement plans in estate planning are covered in more detail in chapter 13

Technically, it is not necessary that each spouse's "basket" of assets be held in a revocable living Trust during that person's lifetime. You could, after dividing your joint tenancies, hold everything individually in your respective individual names, putting shelter language in your respective Wills.

But I'd still recommend revocable living Trusts for all the avoidance-of-probate reasons we detailed in chapter 8. In fact, revocable living Trusts make even more sense here. Without them, the estate will face not just one probate, but two—one for each spouse's basket of assets.

One drawback of shelter Trusts revolves around basis issues relating to capital gains. While a "step-up" in basis eliminates capital gains that occur in the estate of the first-to-die spouse's estate, assets that make up a shelter Trust and grow during the survivor's lifetime do not get a second step-up upon the survivor's death if growth occurs.

Surviving Spouse's Authority over a Basic Exclusion Amount Shelter Trust

The surviving spouse cannot have unlimited power over the shelter Trust assets. If they did, the IRS would consider those assets to be part of their estate and the estate-tax benefits would be lost upon the survivor's death. The question most often asked here is: What are the maximum rights the surviving spouse can have over the deceased spouse's shelter Trust without such assets being included in the survivor's estate? To give the surviving spouse maximum power (but not so much "control" that the shelter Trust is included in their estate), the shelter Trust may include such provisions as:

- Survivor is the trustee and therefore can make all investment decisions.

- Survivor has a right to all of the income from the shelter Trust.
- Survivor has a right to withdraw annually as much as 5 percent or $5,000 from the principal, whichever is greater. This doesn't mean they should make such withdrawals. In fact, if the estate is a very large taxable one, it's generally best that this "five-plus-five power" not be utilized or even included in the Trust. Even if not withdrawn, 5 percent of the principal will be included in the surviving spouse's estate upon their death.
- Survivor has the power, during their lifetime (as long as such gifts are not used to discharge a legal obligation of support) or upon the survivor's death (via an appropriately executed document), to make gifts to descendants of the deceased. The authority to make gifts granted under this type of "limited" power of appointment may extend to gifts to others, such as persons married to descendants of the deceased spouse, the deceased spouse's extended family, charities, and so on, as long as the assets cannot be distributed to the survivor, the survivor's estate, creditors of the survivor, or creditors of the survivor's estate.
- Survivor can receive additional money from the Trust if they are in need. If the surviving spouse spends all their money, including the marital Trust assets; has received the income and 5 percent of the principal of the deceased spouse's shelter Trust (assuming a five-plus-five power is included in the shelter Trust); and still needs more money, the Trust can provide for greater withdrawals, as specified—for example, to be used for the survivor's health and maintenance in reasonable comfort or for emergencies. This provision is designed to ensure the deceased spouse's wish that the surviving spouse's standard of living be maintained.

It is often best to leave the principal intact unless the surviving spouse needs money. Furthermore, if there is an existing marital

Trust, the trustee is often required to deplete that Trust before distributing principal to the surviving spouse.

With larger estates, the odds are good that the surviving spouse will have more than enough to live on, even without any of the funds in the shelter Trust. When a surviving spouse takes money out of a shelter Trust, they might be undermining the estate-tax advantages of the Trust.

Left in the Trust, assets that make up a shelter Trust and any growth or income they produce should pass on to their ultimate beneficiaries free from estate taxes. Whenever possible, in a very large estate, the best idea is to let the shelter Trust increase in value. If successful investments within the Trust have increased from its initial value, say from $10 million to $15 million by the time the surviving spouse dies, then the entire $15 million passes to the descendants free from estate tax, though the assets will be subject to an eventual capital gains tax.

A surviving spouse should take principal from a shelter Trust only when they don't have any other assets to spend or if the survivor's estate is well under the basic exclusion amount. That said, it may be prudent for the surviving spouse to concentrate on investments that grow, rather than produce income, because income retained in the Trust will be subject to income tax, possibly at a higher rate than they would pay if the income were distributed.

Also note that the level of spousal control over the assets in the shelter Trust is discretionary. If the surviving spouse has more than enough to live on without touching the shelter Trust's basket of assets, the Trust can provide the surviving spouse with less authority over the principal or even none.

In this way, the Trust might provide for the surviving spouse if their financial situation became desperate, for some unforeseen reason, but otherwise preserve the assets for the children.

Disclaimer Trust—Creating the Shelter Trust Postmortem

Although the surviving spouse's use of the shelter Trust can be very flexible, it is still somewhat restricted, as assets owned by the shelter Trust must be maintained and accounted for separately from other assets. Also, a primary residence owned by the shelter Trust that has appreciated since the death of the first spouse will not receive favorable income tax treatment upon a sale.

Are there some cases in which you might prefer to make the surviving spouse's control complete? Yes, where a commonality of interests exists between the two spouses regarding contingent beneficiaries, and there is no reason to believe that the surviving spouse will act against the wishes of the first spouse to die.

A couple with a commonality of interests typically has no children other than those they had together; built their estate together; and (absent estate-tax considerations or other special circumstances) intends for the surviving spouse to be the sole beneficiary of each other's estate. If either spouse has children from previous relationships, they usually lack a commonality of interests because the surviving spouse tends to want to leave more assets to their descendants than to the descendants of the deceased spouse. Another example would be when there is a great disparity in age and/or wealth between the spouses, or if there are no children and each spouse wants different ultimate beneficiaries.

In those cases where there is a commonality of interests between the spouses and a relatively minor (as opposed to nonexistent) threat of estate taxes, why not make the surviving spouse's authority complete? There is a way—through the creative and timely use of disclaimers.

This is how it works: Assets are still divided between their Trusts. The sole beneficiary of each Trust is the other spouse. With the correct language in the Trusts, the surviving spouse can disclaim—that is, legally declare, "I don't want to own the assets of that Trust (or a portion of the assets)." Any portion legally disclaimed within nine months of death flows into a shelter Trust with the same authority to the surviving spouse that is permitted in any shelter Trust, except that the surviving spouse cannot redirect Trust assets, during their lifetime or upon their death via the use of powers of appointment. Once the survivor dies, the disclaimed assets must be distributed as if the surviving spouse predeceased the one who, in fact, died first.

The advantage to using a disclaimer is that the surviving spouse can be the one to decide, postmortem, how much money to put into the shelter Trust instead of that decision being made prior to the death of the first spouse. The decision can be based on advice given at that time and based on the estate-tax laws and other circumstances existing at that time.

The surviving spouse may, in fact, not disclaim at all, in which case the survivor owns all of the deceased spouse's Trust assets outright. Or the surviving spouse can still do estate-tax planning by deciding on the amount that is sheltered. This is the ultimate in estate-tax flexibility for married couples with a commonality of interests!

Note that this type of planning may not work as expected if the surviving spouse is, or becomes, untrustworthy or unstable, but if drafted correctly, another trustee may be able to disclaim on behalf of an incompetent trustee.

The Marital Trust—QTIP or General Power of Appointment

You can give unlimited money and other assets, during your lifetime and after your death, outright to your spouse if you are legally married, with no tax consequence if your spouse is a U.S. citizen. However, if you wish to exercise any control over the money after you die, then the gift must be subject to a Trust. If the gift to the Trust exceeds the basic exclusion amount, there are limits on the amount of control you may exercise in order for it to be free from transfer (gift or estate) tax.

Most important, the surviving spouse must receive all of the income from the marital Trust, and the Trust may not be distributed to anyone else during the survivor's lifetime, except at the surviving spouse's direction, if so empowered. You cannot say that the survivor gets the income only until they remarry. That type of provision invalidates the unlimited marital deduction.

If a spouse's basket of assets is worth in excess of the basic exclusion amount of more than $11.7 million, then when the first spouse dies, upon their death, the amount above and beyond the amount put into the shelter Trust may pass into a second Trust, a marital Trust, postponing any estate tax until the survivor dies.

For example, if a couple has a total of $30 million in assets, evenly divided between them at $15 million apiece, when the first spouse dies, $11.7 million passes into a shelter Trust, $3.3 million into a marital Trust. If the couple has *only* $20 million in assets or less, and those assets are evenly divided, then a marital Trust would not be utilized for federal estate-tax purposes.

The marital Trust benefits the surviving spouse and utilizes the unlimited marital deduction. Unlike the shelter Trust, the marital Trust may be structured so the surviving spouse has total control over the assets in the Trust and can withdraw as much as the survivor wants for any purpose.

Alternatively, a marital Trust can be structured as a qualified terminable interest in property Trust, or QTIP Trust, which limits the rights of the surviving spouse. As with other marital Trusts, QTIPs avoid immediate estate taxes by utilizing the unlimited marital deduction. Moreover, the surviving spouse must receive any income that's generated by the Trust during their lifetime and, under certain circumstances, depending on how the QTIP is drafted, may receive some portion of the principal as well.

But a QTIP Trust also preserves the bulk of the assets in the Trust for a different beneficiary after the surviving spouse's subsequent death. This can be useful when, for example, the surviving spouse is a second spouse, and the grantor wishes to support the surviving spouse during the remainder of her lifetime, then leave the money to his children from his first marriage.

Unlike QTIP Trusts, other marital Trusts may give the surviving spouse a general power of appointment—that is, they're structured to give the surviving spouse complete authority to withdraw assets from it. Such Trusts basically become conduits for transferring assets estate-tax free to a surviving spouse, either once the shelter Trust has been filled or when all assets can be distributed to it, if there is neither a control nor an estate-tax reason to establish a shelter Trust. In effect, it's as if assets distributed to the marital Trust are given outright to the surviving spouse. And, in fact, they can be.

Upon the death of the surviving spouse, the estate for tax purposes will include any assets remaining in the marital Trust, as well as that person's own assets. Since there is no restriction on withdrawing the assets in the general power of appointment marital Trust, many surviving spouses during their lifetimes simply transfer the non-QTIP marital Trust assets into their own revocable living Trusts. ●

REAL-LIFE STORIES

Even the best estate plan can be derailed if you don't get around to discussing the details with other relevant parties. Greg and Karen used a shelter Trust in their estate plans to protect a sizable estate. But no one explained to Karen that it's best not to take principal out of a shelter Trust unless she had no other funds available. As a result, after Greg's death, Karen not only lived on the income produced by the Trust, but often dipped into its principal and rarely touched her other accounts, even though they were considerable. When she passed away, nine years later, her heirs found that she had left a sizable estate—but the assets in Greg's shelter Trust had not grown over the years and, in fact, had shrunk. This was a shame because the assets in the account would have been estate-tax free. Meanwhile, much of the saved assets outside the shelter Trust were taxed. This could have been avoided if Karen had consulted an estate-planning attorney after Greg died.

Action Plan Ten: You're Almost Finished!

A four-step strategy to follow up your basic estate plan and minimize your estate-tax liability:

1. If you haven't already done so, complete Questionnaire Two in chapter 3. Use that to roughly calculate your potential estate-tax liability.

2. If you have a potential estate-tax liability, discuss estate tax–saving strategies with your attorney when you meet.

3. If you have already completed your estate-plan documents, immediately begin retitling your assets by contacting your financial institutions and changing ownership of various items. If you are married, this may include dividing your estate with your spouse to maximize the potential benefits of your shelter Trust. At the same time, conform your beneficiary (or secondary beneficiary) designations on retirement plan assets and insurance policies. If you have an irrevocable life insurance Trust, you will also have to change ownership of policies so that they are owned by that Trust (chapter 13). Retitling your assets is a very important step to maximize the potential benefits of your estate-plan documents. Mark a one-week deadline in your calendar to contact all of your financial institutions; note a two-week deadline to fill out your forms and send them to the financial institutions; and then mark a one-month deadline to receive confirmations from all the financial institutions that the changes are in effect.

4. If you have any new real estate deeds transferring ownership to a Trust, file those with the appropriate county within one week after they are signed, or make sure that your attorney is taking care of the property transfers.

CHAPTER 11

Gifting as an Estate-Planning Technique

"Misers aren't much fun to live with, but they
make great ancestors."
—Terry Glaspey

Annual Exclusion Gifts

A simple method for the fortunate few to reduce future estate taxes and for many others to accomplish other estate-planning or personal goals is available to those who plan ahead. You can gift up to $15,000 annually to as many people as you like without incurring additional taxes or the need to file a gift tax return.

This $15,000 gift is known as the annual exclusion gift. The beneficiary of this gift need not be related to you; it can be anyone at all. Sometimes such gifts are made to help friends or family members or simply out of generosity, but they also can be used as an estate-planning tool. Every $15,000 you pass on to your future beneficiaries or others in this way during your lifetime is $15,000 that won't face possible estate taxes after your death.

Two more advantages to gifting:

1. You'll be able to see your beneficiaries enjoying the money while you're alive.

2. If invested, the gifted money's growth takes place outside your
    estate.

Of course, an aggressive gifting strategy will be a serious factor
only if you estimate that your estate will be subject to estate taxes
(unless there are also nursing-home considerations, discussed in
chapter 13), and it will be prudent only if you won't need the
money.

Procrastinators take note: Once a calendar year is past, the
opportunity to take advantage of that year's $15,000 exclusion is
gone forever. You can't just go back later and make gifts for years
you missed. This is an exclusion that rewards those who keep on
top of their estate planning.

If gifting does make sense for you, here are some techniques
you can use to increase its power:

• You and your spouse can each make a gift of $15,000 to the
   same person, or you can make a joint gift of $30,000 (a "split
   gift"), in which case a simple filing must be made with the
   IRS, but there is no tax, penalty, or depletion of the basic
   exclusion amount.

• If the person to whom you and your spouse are making the
   gift is also married, you can make a gift totaling $60,000 to
   the couple each and every year, without incurring taxes or
   reducing your unified credit. In this way, a married couple
   with three married children can reduce their estate by more
   than $1.2 million over the course of a decade without much,
   if any, paperwork.

Gift-tax rates are currently the same as federal estate taxes
upon your death, and if your primary residence is located in a
state with its own estate tax, take advice from a tax professional if
making a gift greater than the annual exclusion amount.

There is one hitch to the $15,000-per-person annual
exclusion: A "present interest" in the asset must be given. A

present interest means that the donee (the person receiving the gift) must immediately be able to use or spend it any way they desire. Such a requirement may be contrary to your purpose in making the gift.

But there are ways to satisfy this rule without giving immediate and total access.

For example, let's say that you want to set up a college fund for your grandchild and donate $15,000 to the fund every year for ten years. You want the money to eventually be used for college or graduate school. Rather than just hand the money over to the grandchild and hope your wishes are respected, you can use any of the following tools:

- A Uniform Transfer to Minors Act account
- A 2503(c) minor's Trust
- A Crummey Trust
- A 529 plan

Uniform Transfer to Minors Act Account (UTMA)

The principal advantage of an UTMA, also known as a Uniform Gifts to Minors Act account, or UGMA, is its simplicity. You don't need a lawyer to establish it. All you need is the child's date of birth and social security number to set up an account with a bank, a broker, or a mutual-fund company titled "[Custodian's name] as custodian for [minor's name] under the [name of your state] Uniform Transfer to Minors Act."

The custodian, selected by you, as donor, administers the UTMA assets until the child reaches a certain age, ranging from 18 to 25, depending on the state where the UTMA is set up. You can name yourself as custodian, but it's not advisable, unless you also name a secondary custodian. If you are the only custodian and you die before the assets are distributed, assets in the UTMA account become part of your probate estate.

Two disadvantages to an UTMA account:

1. When the child reaches the statutory age of payout, they have complete control. You might have intended the UTMA to be used for college, but if the child wants to buy a car instead, they have a right to do so.

2. The UTMA may mess up college financial planning. Under federal financial-aid formulas, children are expected to contribute a percentage of their savings toward college each year, which means that dollars in their name count heavily against them when applying for aid packages.

Minors' Trusts—2503(c)

A second option is the minor's Trust, also referred to as a 2503(c) Trust. Gifts to this type of Trust are deemed to be gifts of a present interest, even though the beneficiary cannot withdraw income or principal of the Trust until their twenty-first birthday or sooner if the donor so provides.

Other requirements of a 2503(c) Trust:

• The trustee must have unfettered discretion to use funds to benefit the beneficiary. For example, the funds cannot be restricted to paying educational expenses. If you select a parent of the beneficiary as trustee (such as your grandchild's father), the trustee cannot use the assets to discharge their obligations to support their child, such as providing food and shelter.

• Once a beneficiary has attained the age of 21, they must have the right to decide who gets the assets upon the beneficiary's own death.

• On reaching age 21, the beneficiary can do whatever they want to do with the Trust assets. Many donors feel that 21-year-olds cannot be trusted with control of a significant sum of money.

One partial solution: The 2503(c) Trust can be set up so that the Trust actually continues past age 21. To satisfy the IRS, the child must be given a window of opportunity of at least thirty days to withdraw the assets, starting on their twenty-first birthday. If the withdrawal right is waived by the beneficiary in writing, then the trustee can continue to control the assets, usually providing for staged rights of withdrawal at certain anniversary dates or ages. At least this way, you don't have to worry about the money once the beneficiary has signed the necessary document.

A less common 2503 Trust is the 2503(b) Trust. A 2503(b) Trust is similar to the 2503(c) Trust, except that (1) all investment income from the Trust must be paid out to the Trust beneficiary as it is generated, (2) the difference between the value of the assets held by the Trust and the value of the beneficiary's income interest does not qualify for the federal gift-tax annual exclusion, and (3) in contrast to a 2503(c) Trust, the principal is not required to be paid to the beneficiary or not subject to withdrawal by the beneficiary at age 21.

Crummey Trust

A third option is a gift Trust with withdrawal rights called Crummey powers, which are also often associated with irrevocable life insurance Trusts (ILITs, covered in more detail in chapter 13), the insurance policy premiums being the amount of the gift in those situations. A Crummey Trust is more flexible than the 2503(c) Trust, in that it may be for the benefit of multiple individuals and can be more restrictive and creative regarding the use of the assets. Incidentally, the name "Crummey" is the name of the family that was the subject of a court case. It does not describe the feeling you get from all of the paperwork it generates.

Crummey Trusts satisfy the "present interest" requirement by giving the beneficiary a limited power to withdraw donations to the Trust in the year the gift is made. Generally, this power is exercisable only during a limited period of time of not less than thirty days each year. The power is noncumulative, meaning that if the beneficiary does not withdraw their allotment during one year, the power of withdrawal over that year's contribution lapses.

Even contingent beneficiaries may be given Crummey powers. But proceed with caution: if the IRS believes that there is insufficient present interest or that there is some collusion or prearranged understanding that the power of withdrawal was never meant to be exercised, it may challenge the gift-tax exclusion of the Trust.

Also, where there is more than one beneficiary, careful consideration has to be taken to avoid a taxable consequence to the beneficiary on the lapse of the power, when withdrawal is not made.

One disadvantage of the Crummey Trust is the need to create a paper trail. Each year when a contribution is made, the trustee must send a "Crummey letter" to the beneficiary advising of the right to withdraw. The Crummey notice is similar to the 2503(c) waiver, except it is done more often if there are annual gifts. This can be a nuisance for those who hate a lot of paperwork.

For a procrastinator, the Crummey's annual requirements can be especially problematic. To make your job easier and to be certain you'll get it done, ask your lawyer for a copy of the form you'll need to send. Make plenty of copies so you can fill in a few blanks, sign, and date them every year, rather than be forced to draft the document from scratch each time.

FLY ON THE WALL

Although the IRS frowns on prearranged or sham transactions, one very popular estate-planning technique is nevertheless somewhat convoluted—the use of waivers commonly known as Crummey letters, in which beneficiaries are saying, in effect, that they understand that they have a right to take your contribution to a Trust or the full amount of their share but decline to do so.

FLY ON THE WALL

The whole concept of the Crummey letter walks the fine line between the IRS requirement for a gift to be a "present interest" and your desire to postpone a beneficiary's full use of the Trust assets. In the vast majority of instances, the beneficiary goes along with the routine, but what if they refuse? There may be subtle ways of coercing a person to sign the waiver. Let's listen in on this totally imaginary exchange between a gifting father and a 21-year-old son who is a beneficiary of a 2503(c) or Crummey Trust that delays the beneficiary authority until he attains age 30:

Dad: "Here, sign this waiver. It says you don't want the money now."

Son: "Actually, Dad, I think I'll just take the money now. I want to buy something."

Dad: "No problem, but if you don't sign, I can pretty much guarantee that you will never get another inheritance from me or your mother."

Son: "Where's the pen?"

The Education and Health-Care Exception

Payments for tuition and medical bills are treated differently from other distributions. Above and beyond the $15,000-per-person gift, you can pay the tuition or the medical bills of anyone you care to without triggering a gift tax, so long as the payments are made directly to the vendor. You can't just give someone money with the intention that they use it for college bills. If you are a grandparent with great financial means, this can be a way to help your grandchildren with their education expenses, while simultaneously removing money from your estate. With tuition at top colleges averaging $30,000 to $50,000 a year and more, such gifts can substantially reduce a taxable estate and help a beneficiary.

Neither room and board nor books qualify for this exemption.

529 Plans

A 529 education plan allows you, as donor, to channel your annual exclusion gift for educational purposes to benefit anyone you wish. There are no income restrictions, and the plans vary from state to state. You can make five years' worth of annual exclusion gifts (currently totaling $75,000) for one person in a single year. If you were to die, however, any "unused" years would be attributed back to your estate. You get no income-tax deduction for making a 529 donation.

However, the income and growth in the plan will never be taxed if used for qualified educational purposes. You can retain control over the 529 account, and you can even change the beneficiary designation if the originally designated person does not use the money. There are generally no age restrictions, so the 529 plan can be used for adult education. For more information, you may also want to check www.savingforcollege.com, a website devoted to 529 plans.

HOW TO DEFEAT PROCRASTINATION

Do not be a perfectionist! Use your best effort at each stage—it's assuredly better than doing nothing at all—and keep moving ahead.

The Big Lifetime Gift

You can make gifts greater than $15,000 per year per person, but such gifts may be subject to a gift tax. Rather than pay a gift tax, most people who make large gifts will use all or part of their basic exclusion amount. Even people who have no basic exclusion amount left often choose to make inter vivos (lifetime) gifts, in order to remove future appreciation from an already large estate.

Choosing the Right Assets for Gifting

As you may recall from the discussion of joint tenancy in chapter 7, gifts of appreciated assets made during your lifetime will be treated differently by the IRS than assets passed to heirs after death through your Will or revocable living Trust.

If you make gifts of appreciated assets during your lifetime—say, giving your child the house you've owned for years—then the recipient may have to pay capital-gains taxes on the entire profit made on the asset from the day you bought it to the day they choose to sell. Conversely, if they receive the house from you after your death, they will face capital-gains taxes only on its increase in value from the time they receive it to the time it is sold, a potentially huge tax difference.

Thus, it often is smarter to make lifetime gifts of assets that have appreciated little or not at all since you purchased them. Leave highly appreciated assets in your estate.

There are three possible exceptions:

1. Assets where there is reason to expect even greater appreciation in the future. If an asset is expected to be worth much, much more by the time you die, it might be worthwhile to pass it along now, even if it has already appreciated.

2. Gifts to charities from non-IRA assets. When giving to charities, an income-tax deduction can be taken for the asset's full value on the date of the gift, and no capital gain is paid. Your basis in the asset is irrelevant, so feel free to give highly appreciated assets to charities during your lifetime.

3. Gifts to charities from traditional (rather than Roth) IRAs. If you are over 70 ½ years old, you can make a qualified charitable donation ("QCD") of up to $100,000 directly from a traditional IRA, instead of taking a taxable required minimum distribution up to that amount. Because no income tax has been paid on the IRA assets prior to withdrawal, you get no tax deduction. ●

REAL-LIFE STORIES

If gifting makes sense because you want to reduce your prospective estate tax, don't put it off. Charlotte, 78, had known for years that gifting would be a good way to decrease her taxable estate. But despite the urging of her financial planner and estate-planning attorney, who saw she clearly had more money than she would ever need, she delayed, concerned that if she gave it away, she might not have enough to live on. Finally, Charlotte's health took a serious turn for the worse.

She decided to make $15,000 gifts to each of her five children and each of her seventeen grandchildren and great-grandchildren, which theoretically removed $345,000 from her taxable estate. Unfortunately, Charlotte died the next day, before any of the checks had been deposited. Because the gift was not completed until after Charlotte's death, the IRS disallowed the exclusions, and the money was still part of her estate, subject to estate taxes. Also, the seventeen grandchildren and great-grandchildren were not direct beneficiaries of Charlotte's Trust, so they particularly lost out.

Action Plan Eleven: Make Someone Happy and Save Estate Taxes!

A four-step strategy for making gifts:

1. Decide if you're certain—not just likely—that your estate exceeds the amount that you and/or your spouse may need in the future. If so, aggressive gifting might make sense. If your estate is likely to face estate taxes, then gifting may have particular advantages.

2. Ask yourself whether the beneficiaries whom you intend to make gifts to are old enough to act responsibly with money. If there is no estate-tax purpose to making the gift, it might be wiser to wait until the beneficiaries mature. If you intend to make a gift soon but do not want the beneficiary to have full immediate use of it, consider using one of the Trust types described earlier in this chapter.

3. If you decide to make annual exclusion gifts up to $15,000 per person per year, whether outright or in Trust, act now. Once a calendar year is gone, the opportunity for making annual exclusion gifts during that year is gone forever. If you are married, consider doubling the size of your gifts. At the same time, consider taking advantage of the education and health-care exception.

4. If you want to gift an amount larger than the annual exclusion amount, remember that a gift-tax return must be filed, and the result will be a depletion of your federal basic exclusion amount until that is depleted, and then such gifts will be taxed. Even then, a reason to do this may be that all growth will occur outside of your estate.

CHAPTER 12

Special Situations and Additional Options

"Oh, well, no matter what happens, there's
always death."
—Napoleon Bonaparte

A well-drafted estate plan must account for unique circumstances. In this chapter we'll take a look at additional estate-planning techniques. Some of these are relatively simple and commonplace, while others are more aggressive, expensive to create, difficult to maintain, and, now and then, challenging even for sophisticated estate-planning professionals to understand.

But don't let that stop you from reading about them. If there's something that sounds interesting but seems a bit complicated, just make a note of it, and remember to discuss it with your lawyer. Don't get hung up and lose your momentum.

The payoff for looking into these additional strategies can be tremendous—if they fit your situation. They can offer additional levels of security, help ensure that your estate is dealt with precisely as you desire, and protect your estate from unnecessary taxes. Uber wealthy people manage to reduce their estate taxes to a fraction of the amount they might have paid without this additional planning.

Who needs to be familiar with these strategies? Everyone from the reasonably affluent (top 1% in assets—say, between $5 million and $10 million) to the super-wealthy billionaires and even regular estates worth a few hundred thousand dollars. They can make sense if you:

- Own a multimillion-dollar life insurance policy,
- Wish to make sizable gifts to charity,
- Own a business,
- Hold a large percentage of your assets in retirement plans, and/or
- Have a larger estate than can be protected from estate taxes even after utilizing the techniques mentioned in chapter 10.

Some other special situations may need to be considered by those who:

- Have beneficiaries requiring special attention,
- Intend to disinherit a descendant,
- Have been married more than once or have children from a previous relationship, and/or
- Would otherwise benefit from additional Trust strategies.

That's a lot of people—and you need to know now if you're among them.

Additional Trust Options and Other Ownership Arrangements

A wide range of tactics beyond those already discussed has been developed for using Trusts and other ownership arrangements to transfer assets. These strategies often take advantage of tax savings, while giving up varying degrees of control at some level. Some arrangements that come in handy are irrevocable life-insurance Trusts, intentionally defective grantor Trusts, buy-sell agreements, family limited partnerships and limited liability companies, grantor-retained Trusts, qualified personal residence Trusts, various charitable Trusts, QTIP marital Trusts, and generation-skipping transfers.

Irrevocable Life-Insurance Trusts—ILITs

It is a common and sometimes costly misconception that life-insurance policy proceeds are never subject to tax. Life-insurance proceeds are not ordinarily subject to income tax, but they can be subject to estate tax if they're within the insured's control.

If you own life insurance outright and your estate, including the insurance, exceeds the federal or your state's basic exclusion amount, it will be subject to estate tax, the same as any other asset.

You purchased life insurance to provide for your dependents upon your death; the last thing you want is to diminish the support the insurance policy was meant to provide. With proper planning, life-insurance proceeds can be removed from your estate. By utilizing an irrevocable life-insurance Trust (also referred to as an asset-replacement Trust or wealth-replacement Trust, or, most commonly, an ILIT), life-insurance policies can provide needed liquidity when estate taxes become due.

An ILIT is a type of living trust that is *irrevocable.* The trustee of the ILIT, who is not you but is named by you in the document, buys the insurance policy on your life with funds that you provide, and the trust receives the policy's benefits when you die. You name the beneficiaries in the ILIT. Upon your death, proceeds of policies held in this manner are excluded from your taxable estate.

To ensure that the insurance proceeds are not taxed in your estate, the ILIT must be irrevocable, and you may not retain incidents of ownership, such as the right to change the ILIT or use the cash value of the insurance policy for yourself. This can be a drawback if you are considering funding the ILIT with whole-life or universal insurance containing cash value that you want to use to supplement your retirement income. For many people, due to its relatively low cost and the fact that it has no cash value until you die, term life insurance is often the primary asset of an ILIT.

Once the ILIT is established, you can transfer existing policies to the Trust, or the trustee of the ILIT can purchase new policies on your life, funded by your annual exclusion gifts of $15,000 per beneficiary (or $30,000 if your spouse is also making the gift).

If you transfer existing policies into the ILIT, you must repay any loans against the policy, or the proceeds may face income taxes. Also, you must live at least three years beyond the transfer date for the IRS to allow the transferred policy's proceeds to be excluded from your taxable estate. With new life-insurance policies owned from the beginning by the ILIT, there is no three-year look-back.

Typically, you, as grantor, will make gifts to the ILIT every year. The trustee, in turn, uses these gifts to pay policy premiums. The trustee gives Crummey notices of annual gifts to all of the beneficiaries. These Crummey notices (also discussed in chapter 11) include advising a beneficiary of the right of withdrawal for a fixed period of time, perhaps thirty days.

Married couples whose beneficiaries could face a cash crunch brought on by estate taxes after the death of the second spouse may wish to consider a survivorship life-insurance policy (also known as second-to-die insurance, death-tax insurance, or legacy insurance).

The survivorship policy owned by an ILIT route is especially appealing if the bulk of a couple's money is invested in non-liquid assets such as real estate or a closely held business, and the basic exclusion amount has been or will be exhausted. Upon a payout, the goal is for the ILIT to provide sufficient liquidity so that your beneficiaries will not be forced to sell illiquid assets at fire-sale prices to pay the IRS or your state's equivalent of the Illinois Department of Revenue.

A survivorship policy can also be useful if a large asset, like a business, is going to one child, and there are insufficient assets to make an equally valuable gift to your other child. All types of insurance can be used to accomplish an equalization, but a survivorship policy is especially suited because of its relatively low cost.

Survivorship life insurance can also endow beneficiaries of an otherwise modest estate. I helped a couple of modest means establish a supplemental-needs Trust for the benefit of their only child, who has Down syndrome. The ILIT was funded by a survivorship life-insurance policy owned by and payable to the ILIT upon the death of the survivor. They bought peace of mind, obtaining a lot of bang for their insurance buck and ensuring to the greatest extent possible that their son's needs in future years would be met if he survives them.

HOW TO DEFEAT PROCRASTINATION

Clarify your objectives. Procrastinators sometimes put off a task because they're not committed to its goal.
Be as certain of your decisions and comfortable with your objectives as you can be, and you'll be motivated to finish!

How much life insurance is appropriate?

- If the purpose of the policy is to pay estate-tax bills so your heirs don't face a cash crunch, base the amount of insurance on the estimated size of your estate taxes. Ask your lawyer to give you a rough idea of how much your prospective estate tax is, and talk to your insurance professional.
- If the life insurance is intended for care of your dependents, the amount to buy should be based on their current and projected future needs. That means enough to pay their day-to-day expenses, monthly mortgage (or to pay it off), car payments, future college costs, and other predictable expenditures.

- If your spouse has a high income, or you have enough saved that your family would be secure even without your income, perhaps life insurance is not necessary.

Establishing and Operating an Irrevocable Life-Insurance Trust

Irrevocable life-insurance Trusts must be handled according to a precise set of rules to be acceptable to the IRS. Frankly, all these steps can be a real pain. Many of those who have them wouldn't have them—except for the considerable tax savings they gain.

Here's what to do for such a Trust to be valid and successful:

1. The grantor—that's you—must send a copy of the Trust to the trustee you selected.
2. The grantor or the trustee must apply for a Trust federal employer identification number.
3. The trustee must open a checking or money market account for the Trust. When the grantor makes gifts to the Trust, the money will flow into this account. The trustee will use this account to pay insurance premiums. Such premiums must never be paid directly by the grantor.
4. The grantor must transfer ownership of the relevant insurance policies to the Trust and designate the Trust as beneficiary of policies transferred to the Trust.
5. If the Trust is to be funded with a new insurance policy, the trustee must sign the policy application and make the initial premium payment.
6. The grantor must transfer any other assets being used to fund the Trust into the Trust.
7. The trustee must send notice to beneficiaries of their Crummey rights of withdrawal in any year when a contribution is made to the Trust. If the beneficiaries are under age 18, the notice should be sent to the child in care of the non-grantor parent and, as a precaution, to a successor trustee named in

the document other than a parent, assuming a parent is the grantor. It is good practice to save the posted envelopes and staple them to the letter, providing proof to the IRS that the notices were sent.

8. The trustee must prepare and file annual federal and state gift-tax returns, if either is required.

9. The grantor must be sure that the Trust always has enough liquidity for the trustee to make insurance premium payments.

10. The trustee must make generation-skipping transfer elections if the Trust uses generation-skipping techniques.

Intentionally Defective Grantor Trusts

Intentionally Defective Grantor Trusts, known as IDGTs, are irrevocable Trusts that exploit certain inconsistencies between income-tax rules and estate-tax rules. They allow you, as grantor, to shift an asset out of your estate for estate-tax purposes, while continuing to act as owner for income-tax purposes. By paying the income taxes, you shift even more assets from your estate.

In many instances, an IDGT is used to "freeze" the value of a closely held business interest or real estate and involves part sale (about 90 percent of its value in a typical IDGT transaction) and part gift (the remaining 10 percent). The sale portion of the transactions may involve the use of a self-liquidating installment note over a number of years, or the note may be payable in installments with a balloon payment on the due date. The IDGT may purchase life insurance on your life, using an interest-only note, with payment of the principal becoming obligatory only upon your death.

Spousal Lifetime Access Trust (SLAT)

A SLAT is an irrevocable Trust that transfers assets from a grantor to their spouse during the grantor spouse's lifetime. The SLAT can be subject to various restrictions that may shield it from creditor claims, along with state and federal estate taxes, and ensure that the assets remain in Trust for the grantor's descendants. It is, in many ways, the equivalent to funding a shelter Trust without waiting to die.

Grantor-Retained Irrevocable Trusts (GRATs, GRUTs, and QPRTs)

An *irrevocable GRAT (grantor-retained annuity Trust)* lets you transfer assets from your estate to a Trust at a discount from those assets' value, "freezing" the value in your estate. By using this technique, the IRS discounts the GRAT below its actual value. Because a GRAT requires considerable bookkeeping and requires that you give up a significant degree of control over the asset, its use is appropriate only for large estates where estate taxes will have to be paid.

There are three requirements for obtaining the discount:

1. The grantor must receive an annuity payment from the Trust for a fixed number of years, based on IRS tables. This reduces the value of the gift to the heirs for tax purposes because the heirs do not have immediate full use of the GRAT assets. The longer the retained-annuity period, the lower the value of the remainder interest that is in your estate.

2. The GRAT must provide that if you die before the end of the Trust period, its assets revert to your estate.

3. If you die before your lifetime benefits are terminated under the GRAT's terms, the GRAT is included in your estate. Conversely, if you outlive the termination date, the GRAT's assets are excluded from your estate. However, if the GRAT is "successful" (you outlive its terms), there will be no stepped-up basis on any appreciated assets, so your beneficiaries may have income-tax issues.

An *irrevocable GRUT (grantor-retained UniTrust)* is similar to a GRAT. The difference is that with GRUTs, assets placed in the Trust are reappraised each year, and the size of the income received by the grantor adjusted accordingly. This might seem like a hassle, but it helps ensure that if inflation takes off, the income the grantor receives from the Trust will increase. That could be important if the grantor is living on the income—but it also could shield less of the assets from estate taxes.

Using an *irrevocable QPRT*, you can transfer your residence to a Trust while continuing to live in it for a preset term of years. You will still be able to deduct your real estate taxes and mortgage interest on your income-tax return. At the end of the fixed term, ownership of the residence passes to the Trust's beneficiaries, often your children. If you, as grantor, wish to continue living in the house at the end of the term, you can lease the residence from the Trust's beneficiaries at the prevailing market rate.

The advantage of a QPRT: Because your beneficiaries receive no benefit from the gift during the term of the QPRT, the QPRT transfer is made at a discount from the residence's existing value for gift-tax purposes. And once the residence is placed in the QPRT, any appreciation in the value of the residence accrues outside your estate.

During the term of the QPRT, you can sell the residence and either replace it with a new residence or convert the sale proceeds in the QPRT Trust to a qualified annuity. If you do sell, capital-gains taxes on any appreciation will be due, although you could take advantage of the preferential Internal Revenue Code rules for capital gains on residences. Roll over any gain from the sale into a new residence to avoid the tax, or use your $250,000 exclusion ($500,000 if married) as often as every two years. The IRS allows two QPRTs per person, so it's possible to use this device for both your principal residence and one vacation home.

A QPRT will help avoid estate taxes only if you outlive its term of years, and then you must rent your home back from your heirs if you intend to continue to live there. If you do not outlive the term of the Trust, the QPRT will be more or less ignored, and the value of the residence is included in your estate.

Like GRATs and GRUTs, QPRTs require substantial paperwork and are worthwhile only if the prospective estate-tax savings are considerable. In such cases, the QPRT can be looked at as a "win-tie" situation. If the QPRT property is included in your estate, your only loss comes from the professional fees associated with creating and maintaining it.

Buy-Sell Agreements

Life insurance can play a role in the estate planning of a small-business owner through a buy-sell agreement.

Such agreements are contracts providing for the sale of the stock of a business upon the occurrence of a specified event, such as the death, disability, or retirement of a major stockholder. A buy-sell agreement often sets the value of the stock or provides a mechanism or formula for valuation.

It can provide a ready market for the sale of the owner's shares by his estate and offer stability to the business by avoiding unnecessary friction brought on by new shareholders. Buy-sell agreements are often funded with life insurance, the proceeds of the policy being used to finance the purchase of the shares upon death.

There are primarily two types of buy-sell agreements.

- A cross-purchase agreement provides that upon the retirement, death, or disability of one stockholder, the other stockholder(s) agree to purchase that person's shares.
- A stock-redemption agreement states that the corporation agrees to buy the disabled, retired, or deceased stockholder's shares.

A buy-sell agreement is especially useful in businesses with restrictive ownership rules. For example, CPA practices can be owned only by CPAs, so a partner in a CPA practice can't leave his wife his share of the business.

TAKING CARE OF (FAMILY) BUSINESS

If you own a business, consider what you would like to happen to it after your death. Is it something you could pass along to a child? Are your children already involved in it, or are they settled in their own careers? Would it be wiser to sell the business upon your death?

Discuss the matter with other partners you may have. Would they be amenable to new co-owners? To working with your children? To purchasing your business outright? A buy-sell agreement might clarify these matters.

Discuss the matter with your children. Do they have both the interest and the expertise to take over the business? Does each child get the same share? What if one child has worked with you for years at the business, while another has not? If you decide that only one child should inherit the business, should the other children get more of your other assets to even things up, or does this child receive the business in addition to an equal share of other assets?

Family Limited Partnerships and Limited Liability Companies

By placing assets in a family limited partnership (FLP) or a limited liability company (LLC), you can maintain virtually complete control over the assets while at the same time make gifts of pieces of the entity to your descendants, reducing future estate taxes. FLPs and LLCs are available in most states, but some state laws governing both are considerably more favorable than others, so don't be surprised if your attorney uses one outside your own state.

Parents may use FLPs and LLCs to transfer such assets as real estate, marketable securities, and interests in closely held businesses to their children. As managing partners or members of the entities, you and your spouse may continue to make all investment and business decisions regarding the assets, but because partial ownership of the entity is given to children or others, valuation discounts of 20–30 percent or more reduce the value of underlying assets due to lack of marketability to third parties and lack of control.

Over time, you can transfer more and more FLP or LLC shares or interests. Using an FLP or an LLC and taking into account discounts for lack of marketability and control, $20,000 or more of underlying value can be transferred, with the gift officially counting as only $15,000. This allows you to get more bang for your annual exclusion buck. Upon your death, the FLP or the LLC may be dissolved and the assets distributed to the beneficiaries.

An FLP or an LLC that aggressively reduces the underlying value of the assets it owns may increase the likelihood of an IRS estate-tax audit upon the death of a partner or a member, especially if it is difficult to see any purpose for its existence beyond tax savings. But if your estate is large enough and the benefit flowing to your family from the use of an FLP or an LLC partnership is significant, it may be a worthwhile technique—despite increased IRS scrutiny.

In addition to using FLPs and LLCs to potentially shelter estate taxes, they may offer protection from creditors. Depending on their structure and the nature of a creditor claim, personal assets may be shielded from claims against the entity at the same time that the value of the entity is shielded from claims against limited partners and members of an LLC.

Both FLPs and LLCs are more flexible than corporations, which must be maintained very strictly to preserve liability protection to its officers or directors. Even if you aren't discounting the underlying assets of the FLP or the LLC, its value for asset protection can still be worth the cost and effort of establishing one.

Charitable Deductions and Irrevocable Charitable Trusts

Lifetime gifts to charities are often deductible, resulting in lower taxes. Charitable donations to charities at death are removed from your estate when calculating estate taxes. The simplest way to make a charitable donation upon your death is to provide for it in your Will or Trust. You may also name the charity as a beneficiary upon your death. In addition, you can utilize charitable Trusts, including the following.

An *irrevocable CRT (charitable remainder Trust)* allows you as the donor to receive the income from the Trust assets during your or a family member's lifetime or for a set period of time, up to twenty years. Upon termination of the Trust, usually upon your death, the assets pass to the charity. This technique works well with highly appreciated assets because capital-gains taxes are avoided.

Assets placed in a charitable remainder Trust are removed from your estate with a corresponding income-tax deduction for the value of the remainder—an estimate of the amount the charity will receive upon your death.

An *irrevocable NIMCRUT (net income with makeup charitable remainder unit Trust)* is a type of charitable remainder Trust that allows income to be deferred to later years. Although the NIMCRUT requires a fixed percentage (at least 5 percent annually) or the income, whichever is less, to be paid to you or some other beneficiary that you choose, the NIMCRUT can invest in assets that, while increasing in value, pay little or no current income. The deficiency between the fixed percentage and the actual income is a tax deferral that builds up over time. Typically, NIMCRUTs are funded by tax-deferred annuity contracts that allow you to defer income until it is requested. If you do not need immediate cash flow, a NIMCRUT may work well as a charitable vehicle with income- and estate-tax benefits.

An ***irrevocable CLT (charitable lead Trust)*** uses the opposite approach from charitable remainder Trusts. A charity or a group of charities receives the income from Trust assets for a set term of years. When the term expires, the Trust assets are transferred to your heirs.

Because a charity receives the income from your assets for a term of years, you are able to pass the assets to your heirs at a discount from the value of the bequest if all rights to the property were transferred at once.

A ***pooled income fund*** is offered by some larger charities. You donate assets to the charity, then receive rights to a percentage of the income generated by the charity's fund until your death. The percentage you receive is based on the value of the assets you donate and projections. Pooled income funds allow you to diversify your assets during your lifetime while benefiting a charity at your death.

A ***family foundation*** allows you as donor to retain personal control and flexibility over the donated assets. If properly established and administered, it can utilize all of the usual charitable income-tax deductions while also providing for the long-term needs of the people and the organizations you want to help.

During your lifetime, a family foundation can become a forum in which family members can work toward a common charitable goal. It can be structured so that, after your death, through good investing, principal may be maintained or increased over time, making an impact for generations to come.

Numerous other techniques, some of which are complex and involve varying degrees of loss of asset control, during your lifetime or following your death, can benefit charities while providing tax breaks and/or income to you or your family. If you would like to benefit a particular charity, it can be worthwhile to approach that charity and discuss creative ways to meet both your needs.

REAL-LIFE STORIES

Forward-thinking individuals, some of whom are only moderately wealthy, set up family foundations to distribute much of their wealth. Joe has a $15-million estate and two young-adult children.

Instead of leaving the children the entire $15 million, he decided to do something that makes sense tax-wise and in other ways, too: He set aside half his fortune to create a family foundation. The children will get involved during Joe's lifetime and help manage the foundation as directors, working with various charitable projects.

This may lead to a greater sense of life purpose than if Joe just gave them the money to buy things or grow the portfolio. It could enrich Joe's whole family in ways that are more important than net-worth statements.

Ask yourself how much is enough. Does it make a big difference if a child gets an inheritance of $3 million versus $2 million? Inheriting large sums of money can sometimes do great damage to a person's character. The inheritor obtains a fortune they never had to work for, then possibly blows it, or—just as bad, in my opinion—the inheritance blocks a natural need to struggle for success, causing a failure to learn about compassion, work ethic, and empathy for those who are less fortunate. Certainly, doing good things for many people can be a greater legacy than just hoarding family money.

Perhaps you agree with Warren E. Buffett, who said it might be wisest to leave children "enough money so that they would feel they could do anything, but not so much that they could do nothing."

What's Best for Charity?

If you want to make asset gifts to charity during your lifetime, you get the most bang for your buck with appreciated assets. This is because you will be able to take an income-tax write-off for the full value of the appreciated asset, but because the charity pays no income tax, it can convert the asset to cash with no adverse tax effect.

In contrast, if you make a lifetime gift of the same appreciated asset to a family member, the person receiving the gift must pay capital-gains tax on the difference between its sale price when the asset is sold and its original value. Plus, you receive no income-tax write-off. When gifting to individuals, therefore, you get the most bang for your buck with cash, cash equivalents, or any asset (such as stock options) likely to grow in the future.

Charities also make great beneficiaries for your IRA and qualified plan assets because these will otherwise be subject to certain income tax and potential estate tax following your death. As discussed in the last chapter, if you are over 72, don't need your IRA RMD, and don't want to pay taxes on them, consider a QCD lifetime gift of IRA money directly to your favorite charities.

THE KRESGE STORY, BRIEFLY

In 1899, Sebastian S. Kresge opened a modest store in downtown Detroit. Eventually, Kresge's evolved into the giant retailer Kmart, land of the blue light special, with more than 1,800 stores and 220,000 employees. In January 2002, Kmart filed for Chapter 11 bankruptcy protection and merged with Sears, another company on life support that is now bankrupt.

Meanwhile, in 1924, Mr. Kresge, with a personal gift of $1.3 million, began the Kresge Foundation, to "promote

THE KRESGE STORY, BRIEFLY

the well-being of mankind." Today, the Kresge Foundation grants support a broad range of organizations reflecting almost the entire array of the nonprofit sector. Since its establishment, the Kresge Foundation has awarded many thousands of grants totaling billions of dollars.

To my mind, this illustrates that generosity can outlast the other good and great things we do during our lives. Leaving a charitable legacy perpetuates your good deeds long after you're gone.

Retirement Plans

The primary purpose of retirement plans, as the name implies, is to provide income for retirement of the account owner. This is accomplished, in part, by income-tax breaks. Money invested in an IRA—or various "qualified" retirement plans, including 401(k), 403(b), and 457 (collectively referred to below as "IRA")—is deducted from your gross income in the year that the investment is made, resulting in a lower income tax. Assets in the IRA grow tax deferred until they are withdrawn.

With a few exceptions if you are still working, you must withdraw required minimum distributions (RMDs) from your IRA prior to April 1 in the year following the year in which you reach the age of 72. Unless you need the money to live on, you want to withdraw as little as possible, deferring income taxes as long as possible. Careful planning will help you accomplish that goal.

RMD rules must be followed precisely to avoid horrendous consequences. Not taking an RMD results in a devastating 50 percent penalty on the RMD not taken.

Upon an IRA account owner's death, a surviving spouse named as beneficiary is considered an "eligible designated beneficiary" ("EDB") who can inherit an IRA and not take RMDs until attaining age 72. After attaining age 72, surviving spouses can stretch RMDs based upon actuarial life expectancy tables.

In addition to spouses, other EDBs are

1. An account owner's child under the age of majority (18 to 21, depending on the applicable state law). RMDs for the minor child must be taken based upon actuarial tables, and when the child attains the age of majority, must withdraw the entire IRA within 10 years. This exception is available only for children and not grandchildren.

2. Beneficiaries less than 10 years younger than the deceased account owner, such as siblings or other family and friends within that age limit, may also stretch withdrawals over their actuarial life expectancies.

3. Disabled and chronically ill (according to federal regulations) beneficiaries may also stretch based upon the actuarial tables.

Inherited stretch IRAs from account owners who died prior to January 1, 2020, are grandfathered, in that RMDs may continue to be based upon the beneficiary's life expectancy. Upon such beneficiary's death, the 10 year rule goes into effect for subsequent beneficiaries. The same is true for subsequent beneficiaries of EDBs. In other words, after the death of an EDB (with the exception of a spouse who rolls over the IRA and treats it as his or her own), the next beneficiary does not enjoy EDB treatment.

When a Trust is beneficiary of an IRA, then if the Trust meets conduit requirements it is disregarded when calculating payout rules for a single beneficiary. The rules for withdrawal by multiple beneficiaries of a Trust are more complex and may short-circuit EDB treatment for beneficiaries that otherwise would benefit from the additional EDB deferral, though there are sometimes steps that can be taken to change the equations. If the Trust does not meet the requirements of a conduit Trust, then the IRA assets may have to be paid out within 5 years after death of the account owner.

Naming a charity as beneficiary of an IRA gives you great bang for your charitable dollar, since neither estate taxes nor income taxes are paid on a charitable bequest. However, mixing charitable and individual beneficiaries of an IRA within a Trust must be done with caution to avoid an accelerated 5 year payout to the individuals.

Beneficiaries can disclaim retirement plan inheritances, charitable distributions can be made with retirement assets, and dividing the IRA into separate shares for each beneficiary are some of the steps referred to above that may realign the amounts each beneficiary receives and remedy technical difficulties that would otherwise force the IRA into a 5 year payout. All such maneuvers must be done on a strict time frame by agreement among the beneficiaries, and if a Trust is the beneficiary, then the trustee must also sign off on the changes.

REAL-LIFE STORIES

When Mark's mother died, leaving him a considerable sum, he made the smart move: he decided not to take the money. This is something that rarely occurs to those who have neither planned ahead nor discussed their options with a financial planner or an estate-planning attorney, but it can make good sense. What's the benefit of turning down a seven-figure windfall? Mark is already financially comfortable, a successful M.D., and has children and

---

REAL-LIFE STORIES

grandchildren. He says he doesn't need the money—but his children might. Also, he is concerned about exposing the inheritance to a potential lawsuit. If he takes the inheritance, it can potentially be laid to waste by a medical malpractice lawsuit, then passed through his estate and on to his kids later—after another round of taxes.

By taking advantage of disclaimers, the inherited funds move on to Mark's heirs, as if he had predeceased his mother. Those considering such a course should note that disclaimers must be made within nine months after the death of the decedent. Both during and after that nine-month period, the disclaiming party must not receive any direct benefit from the assets being disclaimed.

Trust Wrinkles for Complex Family Situations

Not everyone's family is the same. Fortunately, Trusts need not be one-size-fits-all documents. Strategically conceived and properly constructed, they're flexible entities that can accommodate virtually any family circumstance.

Here's a look at some potential complications and how Trusts can be used to sort them out.

Disabled Family Members

If you are responsible for taking care of a family member who will never have the capacity to take care of themselves, your estate plan must address the situation. You can make provisions to ensure that they will have the means to support their current lifestyle without giving them any money outright if they aren't able to handle it or if government aid is a factor.

If the beneficiary is legally disabled and receiving SSI (supplemental security income) or certain other government benefits, a special-needs Trust, or SNT, is essential. An SNT allows a trustee named by you to supplement whatever needs your disabled beneficiary has that are not covered by the applicable social safety net. The SNT is intended not to be used to provide basic food, clothing, and shelter, nor to be available to the beneficiary for conversion for such items, until all local, state, and federal benefits for which the beneficiary is eligible as a result of special needs have first been fully expended for such purposes.

An SNT will give the trustee discretion to pay for the beneficiary's quality-of-life needs, such as:

- The cost differential between a shared room and a private room;
- Travel costs, especially to visit family members;
- Reimbursement for attendance at or participation in recreational or cultural events, conferences, seminars, or training sessions;
- The cost of a companion or an attendant necessary to make travel and similar activities possible;
- Elective medical, dental, or other health services not provided;
- Exercise equipment;
- Computer hardware and software, audio and video equipment;
- Subscriptions to newspapers and magazines and other media; and
- Additional food, clothing, and other expenditures used to provide dignity, purpose, optimism, and joy to the beneficiary.

The payments referred to above are made directly, so they don't disqualify or interfere with government assistance.

Additional instructions may be given to the trustee (or someone the trustee designates) to visit the disabled beneficiary on a regular basis to inspect the beneficiary's living conditions and make certain evaluations, which may include:

- Physical and dental examination by an independent physician and dentist;
- The beneficiary's grooming and overall appearance;
- Education and training programs;
- Work opportunity and earnings;
- Recreation, leisure time, and social needs;
- Appropriateness of existing residential and program services; and
- Legal rights to which the beneficiary may be entitled, including free public education, rehabilitation, and programs that meet constitutional minimal standards.

The above discussion of SNT assumes that it is funded by assets other than those belonging to the beneficiary. If it is funded by the beneficiary's own assets, then it must include language that the government agency or agencies are reimbursed from the Trust upon the beneficiary's death. This type of Trust is referred to alternately as a "payback" Trust or "1st party SNT" or OBRA (d) (4) (a) Trust.

If a person receiving SSI inherits assets in a Trust that threaten benefits, another technique available in many states allows an existing Trust to "decant," making the Trust more restrictive so that benefits are not endangered.

Minor or Spendthrift Family Members

Some heirs are temporarily or permanently untrustworthy with money. In the case of a minor child, it may be just a temporary concern: You don't want to put all the money in the beneficiary's hands until they are old enough to use it responsibly.

A trustee can be given discretion over how Trust assets are spent for the beneficiary's health, support, education, maintenance (HEMS, an "ascertainable" standard"), and best interests. The beneficiary may gain control over the Trust in stages, such as a power to withdraw income at a certain age, followed by a right to withdraw one-half the principal five years later, for example, followed by a right to withdraw the balance of the principal five years after that. You may decide that the beneficiary must never gain full control. The influence you want to exercise from the grave is limited mostly by your imagination and how much you procrastinate.

Even better than granting a right of withdrawal, you can also keep a separate Trust in place for each beneficiary and give them each the right to incrementally act as their own trustees, so that you are not incentivizing the beneficiaries to withdraw money from the Trust until they actually need to use it. Another benefit of this approach is that ownership of an asset by the Trust, rather than individually, provides a measure of protection from non-beneficiaries, such as future ex-spouses of theirs.

Families in Need of Incentives

Provisions may be placed in a Trust to entice beneficiaries to do things you want them to do, such as:
- Go to college,
- Attain a certain grade point average,
- Become gainfully employed,
- Attain a certain net worth through their own efforts,
- Get married, or
- Invite siblings to "life-cycle events," such as marriages, christenings, bar mitzvahs, and other occasions.

Or such provisions may be used in a Trust to entice a beneficiary not to do things, such as:
- Fail a drug test,
- Have children outside of marriage, or
- Pierce their body in various places or cover it with tattoos.

Trusts containing provisions of this sort are occasionally referred to as values Trusts. Some may cringe at such provisions—they are, in effect, telling other people how to live—but some people do that their whole lives anyway. Why stop upon death? When placing incentives into your Trust, make sure that the provisions are flexible because what you think makes sense today may not make sense in the future. For example, if you were to say that children must obtain a college degree to receive any assets, would that be appropriate if a beneficiary became disabled and was unable to attend school? Also, any incentive (or disincentive) provisions should be readily verifiable by a trustee. Having children outside of marriage may be verifiable, while a prohibition on extramarital affairs involves more than a trustee could, or would want to, handle.

Provisions containing incentives usually can be enforced, but the court could dismiss those that are contrary to public policy. For example, a provision that your child not marry someone of a different race would be invalid because it is racially discriminatory.

LEONA HELMSLEY'S UNIQUE INCENTIVE PROVISION

New York hotel and real estate mogul Leona Helmley's Will had many strange aspects (including a $12 million bequest to a Trust benefiting her dog, Trouble), but one incentive provision required her grandchildren to visit their deceased father's grave every year to get a yearly portion of their inheritances.

QTIP for a Second Marriage

As discussed in chapter 11, a QTIP is a type of marital Trust that benefits a spouse during the spouse's lifetime without relinquishing the power to choose the ultimate beneficiaries.

QTIP marital Trusts are commonly used in second marriages and other situations where the first-to-die spouse wants to restrict the surviving spouse's use of marital Trust assets. For example, let's consider a situation where both husband and wife have children from previous marriages. The husband wants to provide for his current wife should she survive him, but upon her subsequent death he wants the marital Trust assets to go to his descendants from his previous marriage and not to her descendants.

A QTIP marital Trust, as with all marital Trusts, requires that the surviving spouse must receive all the income either quarter-annually or on a more regular basis. Upon the survivor's subsequent death, the property is distributed to contingent beneficiaries specified by the first-to-die spouse. The survivor may be given the authority to distribute among a universe specified by the first-to-die spouse, such as children or other family members not related to the surviving spouse. This would be a "limited testamentary power of appointment." If the first-to-die spouse chooses, they can also provide for an unbiased trustee with the authority to distribute principal to the second spouse as needed. Often, a QTIP marital Trust will mirror the shelter Trust, except that in the shelter Trust, income can be retained or paid to someone other than the surviving spouse.

Generation-Skipping Transfers

Above and beyond estate taxes, transfers to grandchildren or more remote descendants can be subject to a tax called the generation-skipping transfer tax, or GST tax.

If you make gifts to a grandchild while the grandchild's parent (your child) is alive, you or your estate will face a highly punitive flat tax of the top transfer tax rate, 40 percent, which is added to any gift or estate tax. This effectively allows the IRS to tax every generation.

Fortunately, there is a GST tax exemption, which is currently the same in any given year as the basic exclusion amount.

There are many reasons to give a gift directly to a grandchild, including an estrangement from your child, the parent. Or perhaps you have plenty of money and simply want to spread it around the family. You can also give a gift indirectly to a grandchild using a GST-exempt Trust. Perhaps your child is in danger of a major lawsuit or has a large estate of their own, does not need your inheritance, or believes it might compound their own estate-tax problems.

Shifting money to your grandchildren might make sense. Using a GST-exempt Trust, you can leave an inheritance under the control of your children (that is, the grandchildren's parents), with the level of control by your children determined by you, the grantor. Of course, if the grandchildren's parents (your children) are in professions where they are at a high risk of being sued, or if they are notably bad with money, it might make sense to name someone else as trustee.

Proper use of a GST tax–exempt Trust is akin to giving your children a gift of an additional exemption from estate taxes. If the money has been invested, the resulting growth is exempt from estate taxes in your child's estate.

An additional technique might be "spray" Trust provisions that would allow Trust assets to benefit any descendant at any level, so that any child, grandchild, or great-grandchild can be helped according to individual needs.

Disinheriting Family Members

Some people decide, often after considerable soul searching, that a potential heir does not deserve an inheritance. It is important that you not just ignore this potential heir in your estate plan. Instead, be very specific. For example, if you are making gifts to all your nieces and nephews, except for one who turned their back on the family twenty years ago, specifically mention that person and your intentions. If they are ignored, they may be able to assert that you "forgot" to put their name in the Will or the Trust.

If you wish to explain your reasons for excluding a beneficiary, keep it brief and unemotional—enough to get the point across without unnecessarily dredging up old conflicts. Best to simply acknowledge it. Something along the lines of "My son, Larry, is not a beneficiary of this estate" is sufficient. Some people get downright mean-spirited when disinheriting, utilizing the opportunity to tell someone "once and for all" what they think of the person. Before you do that, keep in mind that if you commit an act of libel in your Will, your disinherited beneficiary might be able to sue your estate and gain their inheritance (and possibly more) through the back door.

Best practice in some situations is to leave the (otherwise) disinherited beneficiary enough money that, combined with the non-contest clause, they will not cause a problem because they have something to lose.

However, I discourage people from leaving a nominal figure ($1 or something like that) because the insult is generally not worth the administrative hassle of accounting for it.

Disinheriting a spouse can be a bit trickier because many states mandate a certain percentage of the estate for surviving spouses who assert their rights to take a spousal election. Let's say spouses are separated from each other, then one dies and disinherits the survivor. In many states, the survivor can renounce the Will and receive a percentage of the probate estate, typically one-third.

Traditionally, in many states, assets subject to a spousal election were probate assets only. Consequently, many disgruntled spouses structured their estates so the bulk of their assets would pass outside of probate, defeating any spousal rights.

Let's say the first spouse to die has a revocable living Trust. The beneficiaries of the Trust are the children but not the surviving spouse.

The spouse who died first left the following assets:
- A bank account in joint tenancy with a child,
- A brokerage account that is payable on death (POD) to another child,
- Investment real estate owned by a revocable living Trust, and
- IRA and insurance policies that name either the children or a Trust as beneficiary.

In some jurisdictions, the surviving spouse may end up with far less than one-third of the deceased spouse's overall estate. A few states have reformed their laws to allow the surviving spouse to renounce an "augmented" estate, which includes all assets, including nonprobate ones such as insurance, joint tenancy assets, and other assets that would be considered part of a decedent's gross estate for estate-tax filing. Often, a case like this will be decided on the facts unique to the particular situation.

Prior agreements, such as prenuptials, may affect and even defeat a spouse's rights to an elective share. Also, there are technical steps that must be taken by the spouse who wishes to take an elective share, including strict time parameters in which to make a claim.

State laws regarding the disinheritance of a spouse are generally divided into four distinct categories.

First are the states that follow Uniform Probate Code guidelines as set forth in the early 1990s. These states tie the elective share percentage of a decedent's augmented estate to the number of years that the spouse was married to the decedent.

Second are states that disregard the number of years that the spouse and the decedent were married and merely state a spouse's elective percentage in the estate, which may be the probate assets only or an augmented estate.

Third are states that have no elective share statute but allow a surviving spouse to renounce a Will and receive the intestate amount that the spouse would have received had the decedent not had a Will.

Fourth are states that do not recognize a spouse's right to take an elective share. In those states, if it can be shown that the decedent intended to disinherit the spouse, the spouse may end up with nothing.

Mistrusted In-Laws

Perhaps you want your child—and grandchildren, eventually— to benefit from your estate, but you do not want your child's spouse to control a penny of it. With proper planning, gifted or inherited property can be segregated from a beneficiary's marital assets. Not only can you keep the money out of the in-law's hands while married to your child, they shouldn't be able to touch it during a divorce. Make sure you talk to your child or leave a note for them, emphasizing the need to scrupulously segregate gifted and inherited assets from marital assets if this is a concern.

No-Contest Provision

If your Will or Trusts have the potential to make one or more people very unhappy (perhaps you're giving unequal treatment to heirs), consider adding a section to the document disinheriting anyone who challenges your Will or Trust. This will not work on anyone you've disinherited completely; they have nothing to lose.

As a result, it sometimes makes sense to give heirs you would like to disinherit enough of a stake that they will have to think twice before challenging your wishes. A truly devious heir—or perhaps an heir with a good attorney—might find a way to attack the Will or the Trust without triggering this clause, but just seeing the language in the document is often an effective deterrent to a challenge.

These are just a few of the many circumstances that can be accounted for in a Trust. Using Trusts can not only enable you and your family to effectively manage expected circumstances, but also provide help and guidance for unforeseen situations when you're gone. ●

Action Plan Twelve: Make the Tough Decisions!

A nine-step strategy for making difficult choices:

1. Consider whether all of your heirs can be trusted to act responsibly with their inheritances. Decide how much control they should have: Should someone else hold the purse strings? Should your heirs have access only for certain purposes? Should they have access to only a little bit at a time?

2. If you have any heirs who would be better off never inheriting directly, such as disabled family members whose government assistance is contingent on a low level of assets, consider a supplemental special-needs Trust.

3. If there are family members you wish to partly or entirely disinherit, think about your reasons, and spell them out to your lawyer when you meet.

4. If you want to attach conditions to certain gifts, discuss what you'd like to include in a testamentary Trust when you speak with your lawyer.

5. If you are married but have children from a previous marriage, consider how you'd like to divide your assets between your spouse and your children. Speak with your attorney about setting up a QTIP marital Trust, if appropriate.

6. Make note of any additional Trust provisions or other tools from this chapter that could be of use to you.

Action Plan Twelve: Make the Tough Decisions!

7. Determine whether your estate is large enough that estate taxes are a major threat. The "threat" begins at the threshold of your state estate tax.
8. Consider how much inconvenience you're willing to put up with to reduce those estate taxes. Are you willing to:

   - Do some extra paperwork?
   - Do vast amounts of paperwork?
   - Pay large legal and accounting fees?
   - Give up some (or all) control of assets to your heirs prior to your death?
   - Rent your own home from your heirs?

If you're willing to go to these lengths, discuss your options for estate-tax reductions with your lawyer.

Act as soon as possible, especially if you're retired or nearing typical retirement age. Many of these techniques require considerable advance planning in order to be effective.

CHAPTER 13

Maintaining Your Estate Plan

"Spending my children's inheritance"
—Bumper sticker seen on luxury car

Once your estate plan is complete, just a few details remain. With the project so close to the finish line, it's important not to let these things slide—a mistake here can undo a lot of your hard work. Here are some answers to questions that always seem to come up at this stage of the process.

Where Should I Keep My Estate-Plan Documents?

Some attorneys keep all original documents and give clients photocopies or "conformed copies." Other attorneys give their clients all original documents and keep only paper or electronic copies in their files. If your attorney wants to keep the originals, ask about the safety of the location where they'll be kept.

Just because this attorney drafted and even holds the original documents in safekeeping doesn't mean your family is obliged to hire that person if legal assistance becomes necessary in carrying out the estate plan.

If the original documents are in your possession, it's vital that they be stored in a place safe from fire and theft, yet accessible when you die or if you become incapacitated. That may mean either a bank safe-deposit box or a fireproof safe in your home. For many people, especially those with simple, noncontroversial estate plans, just keeping them in a filing cabinet works fine.

If the originals are kept at the bank in a safe-deposit box, a copy should be kept at home so you don't have to run to the bank or call your lawyer when you need to reference the documents. Also, if the safe-deposit box is in your name, the bank might have to seal it upon your death.

It's often better to have joint access to the box with a spouse or another trusted person. The other joint-access holder should have a key to the box or at least know where the key is. Some banks allow for the acting trustee of a Trust to be named as owner on the box, so that if the owner dies, the successor trustee can step right in. Some states seal the box upon an owner's death, even if there is a surviving signer, so understand the bank and state rules when using bank safe-deposit boxes to store your estate plan.

If you use a home safe for your documents, make sure someone you trust has the combination or an extra key. Security experts recommend bolting smaller safes to the frame of the house to prevent burglars from just taking the whole thing with them.

Details of insurance policies should also be accessible. After an exhaustive search of a decedent's files, beneficiaries uncertain whether they've missed any insurance policies can contact:

The American Council of Life Insurance
www.acli.com
Policy Search Department
1001 Pennsylvania Avenue, NW
Washington, DC 20004

Ask for a policy search form. When completed and returned, the form will be forwarded to member insurance companies who search their records and may provide the information necessary for an executor to file a claim on behalf of the estate.

FUNERAL FUN?

Why leave all the planning to others? Marty, known for his casual nature, specified that he be buried in cutoffs, a T-shirt, and sandals and that blues music be played at his funeral.

Amber directed that there be no funeral or wake but instead a memorial service to celebrate her life. There were plenty of good stories, along with food and drink to go around. Her Trust specified that certain out-of-towners be reimbursed from the Trust estate for their travel expenses.

Marge was a world traveler. Next to the buffet at the wake were small ziplock bags with a portion of her ashes to sprinkle at various destinations, along with envelopes addressed to her daughter. Her ashes were spread by Marge's friends and family throughout the world, and her daughter received envelopes from near and far, some with pictures showing the ceremonies that were enacted in Marge's honor. Marge's legacy was burnished even after she died, when her daughter was able to enjoy one last cherished memento of her mom's free spirit.

Even if you don't want to think about these types of creative details, a note or a memo stating your basic funeral and burial or cremation wishes should be kept with your Will and Trust documents. Alternatively, your instructions can be written into your Will.

Should I Discuss My Estate Plan with My Children?

There is little consensus on this point among the experts. It's a matter of your personal family dynamics and comfort level in discussing subjects such as money and death with your children. These can be especially delicate matters when you've decided to make unequal distributions in your estate plan.

On one hand, if everyone, including the beneficiary who receives less than his siblings, knows of your intent, it may be less likely that the one who receives the short end of the stick will cause trouble. On the other hand, some would say that it makes no sense to create problems earlier than necessary. It's up to you.

Should I Consult with My Fiduciaries?

Yes! It's usually best to advise your fiduciaries and other people you name in your estate plan for various roles—that is, your trustees, executors, agents for property and health care, plus (and especially) guardians over minor children—ahead of the time when they will be needed to act on your behalf.

It is also advisable to explain to your fiduciaries the circumstances under which they might have to act. If someone does not want to or cannot act, it's better to know at an early stage.

Some people may be concerned about hurt feelings in regard to the selection of trustee, executor, guardian, and agents. There is no doubt that making these choices is difficult and can cause bad feelings or jealousies. Do not let the fear of hurt feelings prevent you from doing your estate planning or lead you to select individuals who would not otherwise be your first or even your second choice.

HOW TO DEFEAT PROCRASTINATION

Use positive reinforcement to help you maintain motivation and keep working on your estate plan. Frequently tell yourself or write these phrases on paper and post them where you will see them often:
My family deserves my focused attention!
Providing for my family helps me sleep better at night!

How Often Should My Estate Plan Be Reviewed?

You must review your estate plan periodically to account for changing needs and life events. Here are some changes that can serve as an alert to trigger a review with your attorney:

Have your children grown up since you did your Will, so that they no longer need a guardian? _____

Are they now capable of making decisions on their own? _____

Can they now be trusted with large sums of money? _____

When your children reach a point where you'd be comfortable leaving them money, your plan must be reviewed.

Have there been deaths, marriages, births, or divorces in your family? _____

Have you divorced, remarried, or had children since the last review? _____

In some states, a divorce will nullify a spousal bequest unless the bequest is renewed.

Properly drafted documents often provide for children born in the future, but certainly new children are a prompt to make you think about these issues.

Are there family members who have developed special needs?

_____

If an heir is no longer able to care for themself or make financial decisions on their own, the plan must be reviewed.

Have any of your fiduciaries died, become disabled, moved, or otherwise changed to such a degree that they might no longer be able to serve their intended function in your estate plan? _____

If so, your plan must be reviewed.

Is the size of your estate substantially different than it was when the plan was constructed or last reviewed? _____

Check the Value of Your	Value at Time of Plan	Current
Retirement plans		
Stocks or other major investment accounts		
Real estate		
Any businesses owned		
Death benefit of insurance policies		
Art, antiques, or collectibles of substantial value		
Stock options		

If your net worth has increased substantially, you certainly should review your estate plan. Your circumstances might have changed since you and your lawyer last took a look at it, and laws might have changed as well.

Go through the above checklist periodically, perhaps once a year, to see if there is any particular reason to update your plan right away.

Most plans do not require an annual review with your lawyer, but certainly it makes sense to review the plan with him at least every three to five years. Even if nothing changes in your life (other than getting older), the law continually changes. If your lawyer retires, or you lose confidence in them, find a new attorney to do the review. Again, many attorneys will give you a free initial consultation and, either for free or for a small fee, take a look at your current plan and give you comments on how they would update the plan.

Clients often ask if it's okay to update their own plans or whether they need to see their lawyer for even the smallest alteration.

Certain changes can be made on your own, including:

- **Address changes**. If one of your fiduciaries or beneficiaries moves from an address listed in a document, you can probably write the new address into the plan yourself without a problem. But your attorney should be advised so they can update their records, and in any event they may feel more comfortable making those types of changes in a more formal manner.

- **Specific personal property distributions**, if handled properly in the first place. I recommend putting a reference in a Trust to a separate list of assets drawn up by the client. That way, if you acquire new assets (the "stuff" mentioned earlier) or change whomever they're going to, it's a simple matter to make those changes yourself. Note, however, that this informal method is not as ironclad as listing items in the Trust itself and, when used with a Will, carries even less weight.

- **New children or grandchildren**—maybe. If an estate plan is written to account for the possibility of new additions to the family, there might be no need to head to your lawyer every time there's a birth. Discuss this with your lawyer when the plan is drawn up.

From a commonsense perspective, many other changes do require the attention of an attorney. Crossing off or writing in the names of new heirs or changing the percentages that people receive is not something that you want to be in the habit of doing because such informal changes may not withstand attack from someone who feels slighted.

When you meet with your lawyer to review your estate plan, the structure of your estate—how assets are owned and various beneficiary designations—should be reviewed along with your documents.

What Needs to Be Done regarding Social Security?

When you die, your beneficiaries should contact the Social Security Administration (800-772-1213).

Monthly benefits might be available for certain beneficiaries, including:
- A surviving spouse
- Minor children
- Divorced spouses
- Parents who were financially dependent on the decedent

In addition, your estate might be eligible to receive a onetime death benefit of $255, supposedly for burial. If you're not certain that your beneficiaries will remember to call the Social Security Administration, leave a note with your estate plan explaining what to do.

What Will Happen to My Estate If I Require a Long Stay in a Nursing Home?

One of the most gut-wrenching situations that occurs in estate planning involves families depleting their hard-earned assets to pay for nursing-home care.

Medicare may pay for a maximum of one hundred days in a nursing home. After that, people must pay (and pay and pay) until they have depleted substantially all their assets. With the average cost of a one-year stay in a nursing home exceeding $100,000, nursing-home care can quickly drain a nest egg that it took a lifetime to build.

Another government program, Medicaid, a component of the federal welfare system, will pay for long-term care under certain circumstances—but only when the patient has little, if any, money left.

Under current law, to qualify for Medicaid your assets and those of your spouse have to be minimal—no more than about $120,000 in most states. Unfortunately, some people find that divorcing their longtime spouses is the only answer to preserving their estate.

Certain assets, such as a principal residence, might be exempt, but this varies from state to state. In the past, some people have sought to protect their assets and simultaneously qualify for Medicaid by using complex Trusts and divestment strategies to conceal assets. But federal and state laws in recent years have made this very difficult.

Often, people seek to "spend down" their assets to qualify for Medicaid by transferring assets to their children. But when the government determines your Medicaid eligibility, it typically will include transfers made to other individuals or Trusts during the previous five years as continuing to be part of your estate.

Thus, those seeking to qualify for Medicaid without giving up the bulk of their assets must plan long in advance and find a way to support themselves for five years or more with few remaining assets.

WHO IS THE CLIENT?

A type of meeting many estate-planning lawyers dread is with adult children who want advice on qualifying their parents for Medicaid. Besides the fact that various government agencies have tried to put an end to this strategy, there is another problem facing the attorney, namely: who is the client, the parent or the child?

Usually, the client is the person whose assets are being spent down, and without their cooperation, efforts in this area can cause problems for all concerned. A lawyer could in good faith help adult children transfer Mom's assets to her descendants, thinking this is what she would want if she were in her right mind, then wind up in court with Mom saying, "They stole my money," and pointing out the attorney "who helped them."

Another option for protecting an estate from the costs of nursing homes is long-term-care insurance or nursing-home insurance. This insurance can pay for either a nursing home or in-home health care. Like any other insurance, cost of coverage depends on age, health, deductibles, and various limitations.

Long-term-care coverage can be expensive and makes most sense for those who have substantial estates to protect but not enough to handle long-term-care bills out-of-pocket without feeling the pinch—say, those with anywhere from $500,000 to $10 million in net worth.

Will My Estate Plan Be Effective If I Move to Another State?

Estate-planning law is fairly uniform throughout the United States, but there are still many differences among states. In an attempt to unify the various state laws, many states have enacted a statute known as the Uniform Probate Code. This code has been adopted by most, but not all, states.

The U.S. Constitution requires that "full faith and credit shall be given in each state to the public acts, records and judicial proceedings of every other state." This means, generally speaking, that a legal document is valid anywhere in the country if it is valid in the state in which it was signed. So if you have signed a Will, a Trust, or a power of attorney that is valid in the state in which it is signed, it should be valid nationwide and even in other countries.

However, if you move to another state after doing an estate plan, it is prudent to review your documents with an attorney in the new state because no attorney understands the legal nuances of every state. This is particularly true if you move to one with its own estate tax (chapter 10) or to/from a community property (CP) state. Community property states classify marital assets as belonging equally between the spouses, and the planning and asset structures may differ sharply between CP and non-CP states.

Community property states include Arizona, California, Idaho, Louisiana, Nevada, New Mexico, Texas, Washington, and Wisconsin.

What Record Keeping Needs to Be Done with Purchases I Make?

Record keeping can be tedious, but it might be a money saver should the IRS challenge a tax return. Many investors fail to keep track of their assets' cost basis, which is the price they paid for major purchases. When you inherit assets, ask the executor of the estate for the value of the asset at the time of the owner's death and record it. That value is your basis.

If you have failed to keep records, there are ways to find out your basis. For example, if you inherited shares of a publicly traded corporation, your professional financial adviser can find the value of the stock on the date of death of the person who bequeathed the shares to you.

If you were gifted stock, determining its basis is more difficult and time-consuming because you must determine its value at the time it was first purchased. If your financial adviser can't help you, try the corporation whose stock it is or the transfer agent, listed on the share certificate. With their help, it might be possible to determine the stock's basis as of the date of the gift, although a stock purchased thirty years ago may have split ten times and had its name changed or been acquired just as many times. Compound that with shares acquired at various times through a dividend-reinvestment plan, and you have lots of homework to do. It can definitely get confusing!

If the asset is real estate, a real estate agent or appraiser with access to historical data should be able to prepare something for you that is acceptable to the IRS.

Is There Any Other Major Money Planning I Need to Do?

Estate planning does not replace financial planning. A financial plan is a determination of your present and future financial needs and goals and a strategy for getting you there.

Financial planners can provide asset-allocation models and make specific investment recommendations. While financial planning clearly is intertwined with estate planning, you'll be better off asking a financial adviser, rather than an estate-planning attorney, for assistance in such objectives as managing risk or providing a certain income stream.

A financial planner who is not an attorney is prohibited from drafting estate-plan documents. If you use both a financial planner and an estate-planning attorney, these professionals should complement each other's work to give you a comprehensive plan that works for you and your family.

REAL-LIFE STORIES

Gerald, 72, and Martha, 70, had not bothered to review their estate plan in the ten years prior to their death. They didn't think it was necessary: There had been no additions to or subtractions from their family. The size of their estate had not altered significantly, and they had made no major purchases.

But it turned out that a review would have been wise. While their situation had not changed, that of one of their key fiduciaries had: Martha's brother Carl had died. He had seemed the rational choice for the role of trustee because he had been a successful money manager for decades. The couple's backup trustee, Carl, Jr., also was a money manager but had shown nowhere near his father's skill since taking over his father's business seven years earlier. If it had occurred to them, Gerald and Martha would have picked a different trustee.

Don't Delay!

As soon as your estate plan is complete, supply a list of your important documents and their locations to your family and your legal and financial advisers. These likely include:

- A Will (regular Will or pour-over Will);
- A revocable living Trust;
- A durable power of attorney for property;
- A durable power of attorney for health care;
- Any insurance policies;
- A list of assets, particularly those that your heirs might have trouble tracking down, as discussed in chapter 4; and
- Any other important financial documents.

Action Plan Thirteen: Celebrate!

A four-step strategy to keep everything in place:

1. Find a secure place to keep your estate-plan documents.

2. Share the details of this location with family members, and make sure they have access to it in an emergency.

3. Discuss the basics of the plan with your fiduciaries, at least as the plan relates to them. Make changes to your fiduciary designations if there is reason to believe that the people you have selected will not be able to serve adequately.

4. Plan to review the documents at least every three to five years. It's easy to forget things that occur so rarely, so it might help to tie your reviews to some major event that recurs on this cycle, perhaps the Olympics, presidential elections, or years ending with a five or a zero—whatever you feel you'll be able to remember.

Estate planning might not be anyone's idea of fun, but handled properly and with the assistance of a competent lawyer familiar with estate planning and the issues unique to your family, you've probably found that it need not become an overwhelming burden, either.

Congratulations on completing your estate plan! All that remains is keeping the plan up-to-date. If you've come this far, it would be a shame to see those efforts wasted. If you've yet to sit down with an estate-planning attorney, now is the time. Remember, it's up to you: either handle your own estate planning now, or let the government and the courts do it for you the difficult and expensive way. ●

Glossary

"I like to pay my taxes.
With them I buy civilization."
—Oliver Wendell Holmes

2503(c) Trust—An irrevocable Trust established for minor children. Gifts to such Trusts are deemed to be gifts of a present interest and thus can qualify for the annual $15,000 gift-tax exclusion. The trustee manages the Trust assets and, at their discretion, may distribute income or principal to a beneficiary until the beneficiary reaches age twenty-one. At that point, the beneficiary has the right either to withdraw the Trust assets or to leave the Trust intact until a later date. This type of Trust can be a good choice for removing assets from a grantor's estate in favor of a minor while potentially keeping control out of the hands of the immature adult beneficiary.

Accounting—A detailed analysis of income, gains, losses, transactions, and assets that may be required of a trustee or an executor. A Trust and a Will may require accounting for certain situations or might waive the need for it in other situations.

Administration—The management and settlement of an estate in probate court. Similar in usage to the term *probate*.

Administrator (fem., administratrix)—The person or the corporate entity appointed by the probate court to handle an administration when there is no Will or where the executor or the executors named in the Will are unable to serve.

Agent—Under a power of attorney, the person granted the legal right to act on behalf of the principal. Also sometimes referred to as an attorney-in-fact.

Alternate valuation date—In an estate-tax return, IRS Form 706, the executor can choose to value the estate by its fair market value on the decedent's date of death or on the alternate valuation date, precisely six months after the date of death. If the assets have declined in value, this may be a useful tool to cut estate taxes.

Ancillary jurisdiction—A jurisdiction outside the state where the decedent officially resided. If a decedent owns real estate in more than one state, his estate may be subject to probate in each state in which the real estate is located. By retitling real estate owned outside the state of residence into a Trust, multiple ancillary probates may be avoided.

Annual exclusion amount—Each person may gift up to $15,000 per year to any other person without incurring any gift tax. Gifts in excess of $15,000 will result in a partial or full use of the maximum basic exclusion amount and require a gift-tax filing. There is no limit on the number of $15,000 gifts you can make to different people in a year. To qualify for this exclusion, the gift must be of a present interest, meaning that the recipient can enjoy the gift immediately. Annual exclusion gifts are often used creatively to deplete estates with prospective estate-tax problems.

Ascertainable standards—Language describing, and in some cases limiting, how Trust income and principal can be used by a trustee for a beneficiary. A common example is HEMS, an acronym indicating that the trustee can use the Trust's income and/or principal for the beneficiary's health, education, maintenance, and support. If the words "best interests" or "happiness" are used in the distribution standards, they would not be ascertainable.

Basic exclusion amount—The amount that you can transfer to your designated heirs (other than your spouse, which, in most cases, is unlimited) without incurring any estate or gift tax.

Basis—The acquisition cost of an asset, used to calculate gains and losses.

Beneficiary—A person who receives or benefits from a Will, a Trust, or a contractual property such as insurance, qualified plans, annuities, or transferable-(payable-)on-death accounts.

Bequest—Assets transferred to a beneficiary under a Will.

Bond—A guarantee by an insurance company or a bonding agency to repay any loss due to negligence or criminal cause by an executor, an administrator, or a trustee. A Will or a revocable living Trust can waive bond requirements.

Buy-sell agreement—A contractual agreement among partners or shareholders of a business that specifies the terms for buying out one partner's or shareholder's share upon that person's retirement, death, or disability.

Capital gain—The profit reported to the IRS on the sale of a capital asset. Capital gain is the difference between the cost basis of an asset and the net proceeds on the sale of the asset. If the asset is sold for a lower price than its acquisition cost, a capital loss may be reported.

Charitable remainder Trust—The donation of an asset to a charity in which the donor reserves the right to use the property or receive income from it for a specified period of time, perhaps years or even lifetimes. When the agreed-on period is over, the property belongs to the charity.

Codicil—A document that amends or supplements a Will. It must be executed with the same degree of formality as a Will.

Community property (CP)—Community-property states (currently, Arizona, California, Idaho, Louisiana, Nevada, New Mexico, Texas, Washington, and Wisconsin) provide that a husband and a wife each own a one-half interest in the other's community property assets and earnings during the course of the marriage. States that are not community-property states provide for separate property rights during the course of the marriage. In most community-property states, the only separate property is that which is owned exclusively by one of the spouses prior to the marriage and never commingled with community property and assets received by gift or inherited at any time.

Conservator—A type of guardian appointed by a probate court to manage the affairs of a mentally incapacitated adult.

Contingent fiduciary—The backup to the successor trustee, executor, guardian, or agent should that person be unable or unwilling to act.

Contingent beneficiary—The person(s) or the entity that receives a gift if the primary beneficiary is then deceased.

Crummey power—The right of a donor to make gifts to a Trust with a withdrawal right. The donor or the trustee must notify the beneficiary of his Crummey rights to withdraw some or all of the value of the gift in the year made. The right to withdraw—which is typically not exercised—is required for the donation to the Trust to be a gift of a present interest.

Custodian—The person or the organization managing assets for minor children or adults deemed incompetent.

Death probate—The process of legally validating a Will or an intestate estate. It involves collecting assets, paying bills, and eventually retitling the assets, all under the supervision of the probate court. For living probate, see "Guardianship." Many types of probate can be substantially avoided and its costs minimized though proper estate planning.

Decedent—A person who has died, whether testate or intestate (that is, with or without a Will).

Descendant—A person who is a relative in a direct vertical line from another person—children, grandchildren, great-grandchildren, and so forth.

Disclaimer—A person inheriting assets can refuse to accept any or all of those assets. Disclaimers can be very useful in certain situations, especially if they have been anticipated and planned for. An effective disclaimer is governed by strict state and federal laws. Among other things, a disclaimer must be in writing and made within nine months of a person's death.

Domicile—The state or the county where a person primarily resides, determining the taxing and probate jurisdictions.

Donee—A person who receives a gift or a bequest or to whom a power of appointment is given.

Donor—See **Grantor**.

Durable power of attorney—See **Power of attorney**.

Escheat—The process by which assets of a person who dies intestate (without a Will), without heirs, go to the state.

Estate tax—A transfer tax that the federal government and some states assess on the right to transfer assets to others on your death. Often referred to as the death tax or, sometimes incorrectly, as inheritance tax.

Executor (archaic fem., executrix)—A person, a bank, or a Trust company designated in your Will to administer your estate upon your death, under the supervision of the probate court. More than one executor can act together as co-executors. Referred to in some states as a personal representative.

Family Limited Partnership (FLP)—A legal entity created by state statute that serves estate planning, asset protection, and business continuity needs.

Fiduciary—A person in a position of trust and responsibility, subject to heightened legal and ethical standards, including, among others, trustees, executors, guardians, and agents.

Generation-skipping transfer tax (GST tax)—An additional transfer tax assessed on gifts and bequests in excess of the basic exclusion being distributed among grandchildren, great-grandchildren, or anyone at least two generations below the donor. Language allocating an exemption from the tax can be included in a generation-skipping tax exempt Trust as part of the overall Trust.

Gift—A voluntary transfer of property to another person made without receiving something of equal value. A completed gift, which removes an asset from a donor's estate, must be of a present interest and without any conditions. The federal government will assess a gift tax when the value of the gift exceeds the annual exclusion if the basic exclusion amount has been exhausted.

Grantor—The person who establishes a Trust and transfers their own assets to it. Also called the trustor, the settler, or the donor.

Grantor Trust—A Trust in which the grantor retains control of the assets or the income. The income from a grantor Trust is taxable to the grantor, rather than to the beneficiary, although the grantor and the beneficiary may be one and the same.

Guardian—The person appointed by a probate court, often designated in your Will, to be responsible for your children or an incompetent adult. In the case of the incompetent adult, also known as a conservator.

Guardianship—The probate court process of administration or management of the property or the person of minor children and incompetent adults, a type of living probate. Guardianships of incompetent adults can generally be avoided though the use of Trusts and durable powers of attorney if signed while the person is still competent.

Heirs—The persons who would receive your probate assets without a Will.

Incidents of ownership—Any element of control or ownership rights in an asset that causes it to be includible in an estate for estate-tax purposes.

Incompetence—The inability of a person to function and take care of their own affairs, sometimes referred to as a legal disability or incapacity.

Inheritance tax—A tax levied by some states on the right of heirs to inherit assets. An inheritance tax differs from an estate tax because it is imposed on the heir, rather than on the estate, and often differs based on the legal relation of the heir to the decedent.

Intentionally defective grantor Trust (IDGT)—Income tax–shifting Trust, in which a grantor irrevocably transfers assets, usually by partial gift and partial sale, out of their estate but still pays the income taxes on earnings and capital gains, even though paid to the beneficiaries.

Inter vivos Trust—A Trust created during your lifetime, often, though not always, equivalent to a revocable Trust.

Intestate—Dying without a valid Will; the probate court will determine who receives your assets, following state intestacy laws.

Inventory—A list of all assets contained in a probate estate. A probate estate inventory is a matter of public record, available for examination by anyone who cares to request it.

Irrevocable Trust—A Trust that cannot be amended or revoked by its grantor. Like corporations, these are separate tax entities. Irrevocable Trusts are often used in estate planning to place assets outside of someone's estate during that person's lifetime. One of the most common types of irrevocable Trusts created during lifetime is the irrevocable life-insurance Trust (ILIT), which is intended primarily to prevent insurance death benefits from being included in your taxable estate. All Trusts that continue after a person has died are irrevocable, though the word must not be confused with "inflexible" because an irrevocable Trust can, depending on its terms, be malleable in the hands of the trustee and the beneficiaries.

Joint tenancy with right of survivorship (JTWROS)—Shared ownership between two or more people, with the survivor(s) owning the property after the death of one or more fellow joint tenants. This delays probate but ultimately does not avoid it.

Moreover, it may result in income- and estate-tax pitfalls, along with unintended liabilities. Compare with **Tenancy in common**.

Legacy—Property transferred by your Will. The person receiving a legacy is the legatee. It is also the immeasurable sum of your life influences.

Letters testamentary—Term used in some jurisdictions to refer to the legal document that provides the proper authority for an executor to act for the estate of a deceased person. Also referred to as "letters of office."

Limited liability company (LLC)—A legal entity created by state statute that serves estate-planning, asset-protection, and business-continuity needs.

Living Trust—A Trust created during the lifetime of the grantor. A living Trust may be revocable or irrevocable.

Living Will—A statement of philosophy concerning your desire to end treatment in the case of extreme injury or illness, if the procedures in question are only going to delay the dying process. The living Will is generally considered a less important health-care directive than the health-care power of attorney.

No-contest clause—A clause in some Wills and Trusts that purports to disinherit any person attempting to attack the validity of such Will or Trust. Does this work? Sometimes, depending on the court and the equities involved. If the beneficiary is receiving an inheritance, even if substantially less than others, and therefore has something substantial to lose, it may at least give them pause before contesting the document, unlike a disinherited person, who may have nothing to lose by contesting just to throw a wrench into the transfer process. Also known in Latin as an "In terrorem" clause.

Payable-on-death account (POD)—A type of bank or brokerage account that avoids probate by naming beneficiaries. If a person has a limited net worth and beneficiaries with no complicating factors, this may be a useful tool. Also referred to as a transfer-on-death account (TOD).

Per capita—A distribution made equally to a number of persons without regard to generation. A distribution to "all my descendants equally and per capita" would result in children, grandchildren, and great-grandchildren each receiving the same amount. This is generally a less prevalent distribution pattern than per stirpes distributions.

Per stirpes—Latin for "by the branch," the method of dividing assets among descendants so that such descendants as a class take the share that a deceased ancestor/beneficiary would have been entitled to take had the ancestor survived.

Portability—Preserving the unused basic exclusion amount of a deceased spouse in an estate tax return.

Pour-over Will—A Will used in conjunction with a revocable living Trust stating that all probate assets are to be transferred ("poured over") to the Trust. Even where there is a fully funded Trust, you should have a pour-over Will to connect future unaccounted probate assets to the Trust.

Power of appointment—The right of a beneficiary to transfer or dispose of Trust assets that the beneficiary does not own outright. If estate-tax planning is involved, care must be taken that the power is not a general power, in which case the assets subject to the power may unintentionally be included in the estate of the person who has the power. A special power limits the authority of the person holding the power to transfer assets, perhaps restricting transfers to a particular class of persons, such as to the descendants of the original donor or to charities. If the trustee has discretion to appoint to themselves, then lacking ascertainable standards, the power of appointment is a general one.

Power of attorney for health care—Document allowing your agent to direct your health care if you are unable to do so, potentially avoiding a guardianship of the person.

Power of attorney for property—A document in which you grant an agent the authority to handle financial matters, either immediately or upon some contingency, such as a future incapacity. The document is used to avoid a financial guardianship proceeding in court, which is a type of living probate.

Precatory language—Suggestive language in a Will or a Trust that expresses your sentiments or preferences but is not binding.

Principal—(1) The assets that make up a Trust, sometimes referred to as the corpus. Many Trusts provide for separate treatment of principal and income derived from the principal. (2) The person who confers authority on an agent in a power of attorney.

Probate—See **Death probate**.

Probate assets—Assets that do not effectively transfer to a surviving joint tenant or via a beneficiary designation or another written agreement and are not owned by a Trust.

Probate court—A state court where probate estates are administered. In some jurisdictions, a magistrate's court or a surrogate court handles probate functions.

Qualified domestic Trust (QDOT)—Special language that must be part of the marital Trust portion of a revocable Trust to transfer Trust assets to a non–U.S. citizen surviving spouse.

Qualified S corporation Trust (QSST)—A Trust that contains special provisions to enable it to own subchapter S corporation stock.

Qualified terminable interest in property Trust (QTIP)—A type of marital Trust that qualifies for the unlimited marital exclusion but does not give the surviving spouse a general power of appointment. QTIPs limit the rights of the surviving spouse in such a way that the assets are preserved for beneficiaries upon the surviving spouse's subsequent death. As with any marital Trust, the surviving spouse must receive all of the Trust's income during their lifetime and can, under certain circumstances, also receive portions of principal. This can be especially useful where there is a second marriage and the grantor wishes to protect the children from the first marriage while benefiting the surviving spouse during the survivor's lifetime.

Remainder—The assets remaining in an estate for a beneficiary or an heir, after an income or other temporary interest has ended.

Residuary—The assets remaining in an estate after all specific transfers of property are made and all expenses are paid. Generally, a pour-over Will pays the residuary to a Trust.

Retitling—(1) The process that legally transfers ownership of property from the grantor to the revocable living Trust. Without retitling assets, a revocable living Trust is unfunded and will not work efficiently as a means to avoid probate. (2) The portion of the probate process that, at the court's direction, transfers ownership of assets from the decedent to the heirs or the beneficiaries.

Revocable living Trust/revocable Trust—A Trust established by the grantor during their lifetime that can be amended (changed) or revoked (canceled) at any time while the grantor is living and competent. Sometimes called an inter vivos (Latin for "while living") Trust, also interchangeable with "revocable Trust" and "living Trust," though a living Trust can also be irrevocable.

Rule against perpetuities—A common-law principle that prevents a person from reaching out from the grave to control his assets forever. A Trust interest must vest not more than "twenty-one years plus a life in being." The movie *Body Heat* shows William Hurt's character flummoxed by the rule. In recent years, many states have, by statute, enacted laws enabling people to set up their estates so as to bypass the rule.

S corporation—A corporation whose income is paid directly and taxed to its shareholders, thus avoiding a corporate tax. Only certain Trusts may own S corporation shares.

Self-declaration of Trust—A type of revocable living Trust in which the grantor is also the trustee and therefore controls the assets of the Trust. During the grantor's lifetime, this type of Trust is generally not a tax entity. Rather, the EIN number is usually the grantor's social security number.

Settler—See **Grantor**.

Shelter Trust—A Trust designed to protect the basic exclusion amount that each person may gift or bequeath to heirs. Between spouses, this is often referred to as a bypass Trust because the Trust assets more or less bypass the surviving spouse and are not included in the survivor's estate. Still, the surviving spouse can have certain rights in the Trust during their lifetime. It also is referred to as the "B" Trust in an "A-B" Trust.

Spendthrift provision—A clause in a Trust that prevents a beneficiary from spending an inheritance without restraint and also may prevent the beneficiary's creditors from reaching the beneficiary's interest in the Trust.

Sprinkle power—A trustee's right to distribute income in any proportion to several named beneficiaries. Such a power gives the trustee the discretion to distribute money according to the relative needs of the beneficiaries.

Stepped-up basis—The rule that makes an heir's cost basis equal to the value of the asset at the date of the grantor's death—or, alternatively, six months later—rather than its original cost. If a gift of an appreciated asset is made during the donor's lifetime, the donee takes the donor's original cost basis, and there is no step-up in the basis. The step-up avoids a capital-gains tax on the appreciation that occurred during the donor's lifetime.

Successor trustee—Under a self-declaration of Trust, the backup to the grantor, who is often the initial trustee. The document can provide for successors to act individually or collectively. The same holds true for other fiduciaries, such as executors of a Will and agents under powers of attorney, so that if one cannot act, another fiduciary steps in and takes their place.

Survivorship insurance—A life-insurance policy that insures a couple, instead of an individual. It can be much less expensive than an individual insurance policy. One of its purposes is to pay the estate taxes that arise after the death of a surviving spouse; it is most useful where the decedent's assets are predominantly illiquid, such as real estate or a family business. In order to be properly utilized, the policy should be held outside the insured couple's estate, possibly in an irrevocable insurance Trust (ILIT). Also commonly referred to as a second-to-die policy.

Tangible personal property—Movable property such as jewelry, clothing, automobiles, and so on, as opposed to real property (land and buildings) or intangibles such as stocks, bonds, and bank accounts.

Tenancy by the entirety—A cousin to joint tenancy ownership, available in some states for a husband and a wife who own real estate, it protects the property from creditors and liability claims against one of the spouses. As with a joint tenancy, this delays but does not eliminate probate, though some states allow tenancy by the entirety using Trusts.

Tenancy in common—An undivided interest in property. Unlike a joint tenancy interest, there is no right of survivorship to the remaining tenants in common. Different types of entities may be tenants in common. If the tenant in common who dies is an individual, there may be a need to probate. Property also may be owned by more than one Trust as tenants in common.

Testamentary Trust—A Trust created under a Will or a revocable Trust and activated upon death. If created as part of a Will, it does not necessarily avoid probate. All testamentary Trusts are irrevocable.

Testator (archaic fem., testatrix)—A person who creates and executes a valid Will.

Trust—A legal written arrangement in which one or more trustees hold and manage assets for the benefit of one or more beneficiaries under a fiduciary relationship.

Trustee—The person or the company acting in a fiduciary capacity, managing and administering Trust assets for the benefit of one or more beneficiaries.

Trustor—See **Grantor** and **Settler**.

Uniform Transfers to Minors Act (UTMA)—A method of holding property for the benefit of a minor. It is simple to set up but less flexible than a 2503(c) Trust or a Crummey Trust.

Unlimited marital deduction—A rule permitting spouses to transfer an unlimited amount of assets to each other, while alive or after death, without any income-tax or estate-tax implications. Overuse of the unlimited marital deduction may lead to a loss of the basic exclusion amount of the first spouse to die.

Will—A legal document completed in accordance with state law that lays out how your assets will be distributed upon your death. The Will appoints an executor to administer your estate and may establish testamentary Trusts for children. It may also name guardians for minor children.

Will contest—A legal challenge to a Will, usually made by one or more disgruntled heirs, which can result in great expense to the estate and tie up the estate for prolonged lengths of time. Will contests often are based on allegations that the Will was improperly executed or that the decedent lacked proper mental capacity at the time they created the Will or that someone exerted undue influence on the decedent.

Index

AUTHOR PROFILE

Eric G. Matlin is the founding partner of Matlin Law Group, P.C., in Northbrook, Illinois. He has worked with thousands of families on their estate plans. His clients range from people with a negative net worth to people with well over $10 million in assets. He lives with his wife, Glo, and their goldendoodle, Maizie. His children are grown and out of the house.

For more information, visit the Matlin Law Group, P.C., website at www.MatlinLawGroup.com.

Made in the USA
Monee, IL
10 July 2021

72549481R00144